ON THESE
COURTS

A MIRACLE SEASON THAT CHANGED A CITY,
A ONCE-FUTURE STAR, AND A TEAM FOREVER

WAYNE B. DRASH

A Touchstone Book

Published by Simon & Schuster

New York   London   Toronto   Sydney   New Delhi

Touchstone
A Division of Simon & Schuster, Inc.
1230 Avenue of the Americas
New York, NY 10020

First Touchstone hardcover edition May 2013

For information about special discounts for bulk purchases,
please contact Simon & Schuster Special Sales at 1-866-506-1949
or business@simonandschuster.com.

The Simon & Schuster Speakers Bureau can bring authors to your live event.
For more information or to book an event contact the Simon & Schuster Speakers
Bureau at 1-866-248-3049 or visit our website at www.simonspeakers.com.

Designed by Akasha Archer

Manufactured in the United States of America

10 9 8 7 6 5 4 3 2 1

Library of Congress Cataloging-in-Publication Data

Drash, Wayne B.
  On these courts : a miracle season that changed a city, a once-future star, and a
team forever / by Wayne B. Drash.
     pages cm.
1. Hardaway, Anfernee. 2. Basketball players—United States—Biography. 3.
Orlando Magic (Basketball team) I. Title.
  GV884.H24D73 2013
  796.323092—dc23
  [B]
                                  2013000520

ISBN 978-1-4767-1021-1
ISBN 978-1-4767-1025-9 (ebook)

For Malcolm, Macio, and Arvin

Contents

Binghampton, stand up!

The Run

The crowd, a mix of pimps, dealers, moms, middle school teachers, and neighborhood kids, followed the white Cadillac Escalade along Carpenter Street. All wanting to congratulate the boy who had returned a man and brought some actual good news to Binghampton. A place known more for killings and drive-bys than feel-good news stories. Residents joke that the local TV stations use a red dot—*for blood*—to locate their neighborhood on maps.

Out of the SUV stepped Coach Penny.

The No. 3 pick in the NBA in 1993, Penny handed boxes from the back of the Escalade to Coach Dez and Penny's cousin LaMarcus Golden. Inside the boxes were pens and pads of paper for the dozen boys waiting in the Lester locker room. The Lester Lions had lost two consecutive games over Christmas break, a losing streak that threatened to ruin the season. The team responded with two quick wins. Yet in the recent wins, Lester showed dominance early on but a lack of leadership in clutch time.

With the team now holding a respectable 13-3 record, Penny reminded them that a middle school team from Memphis had never won the small division championship. He pointed at the players sitting before him, told them they had the talent to conquer the title. Focus on that larger goal. That's what you do in life—move beyond a hiccup and collect yourself.

"Y'all have an opportunity to make history right now," Penny began. "We're not gonna let you mess up."

His voice echoed off the yellow cinder-block walls. In the room with the boys was perhaps the most talented staff ever to coach middle school. Joining the former NBA all-star and Coach Dez, who had been a standout player himself, was Penny's cousin La-Marcus, a University of Tennessee star who played professionally overseas and for the Harlem Globetrotters. These were ballers, now turned coaches, determined to make a difference.

Penny apologized to players who didn't get as much playing time over the holidays. The games had tightened. Lester was no longer routing teams by 50 points. The starters carried the load. Coach Penny sought to calm any tensions.

"We've got your back. We don't want you to be unhappy. We want you to be a part of the team. But you've gotta know the plays, you gotta know what to do in every situation.

"From the last person on the team to the first person," Penny said, "we need everybody. Everybody!"

The other boys nodded their heads. Coach Dez did, too. Penny might've dazzled on the court as a player, but he was even more electrifying as a coach. His speech had just enough tenacity, mixed with inspiration, to grab the boys by the collar, to make them want to do better.

"When I go home at night and y'all chill," Penny continued, "I sit at home and figure out ways for us to win. We don't just leave here and say forget the team. I go home and I do homework on you, because I am trying to figure out how we can win. We're trying to win the state. Now, what are our weaknesses?"

Not a single voice spoke up.

"You can't think of a weakness?" he asked.

To understand what it takes to be a champion, Penny declared, you have to first understand yourself. The team must know "what we're good at and what we're bad at. Once you understand that, then we can teach you what we want to work on."

Nick Merriweather bobbed his head. The egos on the team had grown bigger and bigger with each early win. When they played Penny's former high school team, Treadwell (now a Memphis middle school), Lester beat them by more than 60 points. Players and fans alike laughed at the beating.

But the consecutive losses over the holidays put a challenge to the team. They'd been humbled. Yes, Lester had rebounded with two wins. It was time to seize on that momentum. Put the pedal to the metal. Don't let up. Make Binghampton proud.

Penny knew a championship wouldn't be given to them, that their opponents would not gift-wrap the title. For now, the team needed to refocus and get back to the basics. He also knew championships can slip away. For all his accomplishments in basketball, Penny had never won that big trophy. He'd come up short in high school, college, and the NBA. In 1996, he'd worn a gold medal around his neck at the Summer Olympics in Atlanta as a member of what was known as Dream Team III. As glorious as it was to win the gold medal, it offered a mere taste of the championships he hoped to win. Penny was just three years into his pro career. He had loftier ambitions: multiple NBA titles. Yet they never came.

Now, in front of the Lester boys, Penny took out a piece of chalk and wrote WEAKNESSES. "I've got nine."

Penny went down the list like it was groceries:

1. Ballhandling
2. IQ of the game
3. Free throws

"When we get on you, it's not because we don't love y'all," he said. "This is how you find out about yourself. This is how you find out about how your teammates think. This is how you find out how your coaching staff thinks."

4. Turnovers
5. Size: We're small
6. One-on-one defense

Penny turned directly to Reggie and Robert. It's a difficult task to manage players as a coach, and when you have two middle schoolers hoping to become the next legend of Binghampton, it gets exponentially more difficult. Both Reggie and Robert competed more among themselves than they did against the opposing team. Penny felt they had slacked off over Christmas break. They might be the team's biggest stars, but they weren't giving everything they had—a failure that Penny admitted reflected poorly on the coaching staff. At 6-foot-3 and 6-foot-4, they should rule every trip up court.

"We need to teach you to play more than a quarter," Penny said. "You play hard. It's just that we want more. We want the best of the best. We want to be fair about that as coaches. But we want you to be the best you can be."

7. Speed: We're slower than most teams

8. Team help on defense

9. Pressure denying the ball

"The best you can be." Those words settled among the lockers.

"Guess how many strengths I got?"

"Three," called guard Kobe Freeman.

"One," Penny replied. "I've got one strength and nine weaknesses. What's that tell y'all?"

He didn't wait for a response. "We're not reaching our potential. We've beaten teams because we got better players than they do, we got more players than they do. That's why we beat them.

"We gotta teach y'all what we want."

On the board, he wrote STRENGTHS, followed by only one example:

We pass the ball well.

By now the speech had lasted fifteen minutes. The players started to drift, almost as if they were in math class.

"We're not done yet. I wanna keep talking," Penny said.

At 6-foot-7, Penny towered over the boys, even the stars. "Who wants to win the state?" he asked.

One by one, Reggie, Robert, Nick—and everyone else in the locker room—raised their hands. "That's good to know," Penny said.

He spoke of staying composed, of containing their emotions when rough times hit. In the games Lester lost, Penny noted, there was too much hollering among teammates.

"There's gonna be ups and downs. We're so used to beating everybody—we jump on everybody," he said. "But once we got down ten points, we just started giving up. Y'all started arguing. We can't do that.

"Stay together! We're the only ones who can stop us. What do we say every time? We say, 'Play hard and play smart.'"

Binghampton hadn't seen a team this talented since the Reagan administration. "Been twenty-seven years," Coach Dez said. And even then, the school didn't win the championship.

"Do you know how big that is?" Penny said, smiling. "Y'all might get free Burger King if we win this thing."

Finally, he finished talking. The boys huddled around. They placed their hands on top of one another. The team was led in their chant by the Lion's hype man, Kobe.

"One, two, three!" they shouted. "One for all, all for one, all for Lester!"

Two final words—THE RUN—stared down from the chalkboard.

CHAPTER I

The Curse of the Assassination

The skinny 6-foot-2 kid looked like the basketball version of a beanpole. He was rail thin, maybe 160 pounds, still baby-faced with a fade haircut. But he had mad skills. He drained three-pointers. He used a crossover to free space and then stepped back to shoot fallaway jumpers over older players. He took the big guys inside and faced them up.

I was watching from the sidelines of Memorial Coliseum, the vaunted arena along the Avenue of Champions in Lexington, Kentucky. The mecca of college basketball, where the University of Kentucky's Adolph Rupp once roamed the sidelines in suit and tie, a scowl like a rattlesnake across his face. On this floor, Kentucky won two national titles. The Wildcats compiled an incredible 307–28 record in the gym over twenty-six seasons, beginning in 1950. It was here where legends were made.

It was June 1987 and I was an equally skinny kid with a tight buzz cut, less focused on the history of the place and more focused on who would make the best player on my Eddie Sutton basketball camp team. As soon as I saw those moves I desperately wanted to get him on my team. I was able to zero in on the gifted shooter amid the packed auditorium of kids with flattops and ludicrously tight 1980s basketball shorts from around Kentucky, Tennessee, and other states.

I need that guy on my team.

At fifteen, I was entering my sophomore season of high school. I was no slouch, having averaged 25 points a game as an eighth grader, which got me a tour of the campus of the University of Arkansas, a trip that ended with me standing at the center of Barnhill Arena, an assistant coach at my side, his arm draped over my shoulder. "Imagine this place packed with ten thousand people," said Mike Anderson, the right-hand man of head coach Nolan Richardson. "The game is on the line. Everyone standing, chanting, 'Drash! Drash! Drash!'" I hoped to be the white guy on the 40 Minutes of Hell team.

Yet my freshman year—marked by a move to a new town and a lousy season—promptly reined in my basketball expectations. I came to Lexington to try to restore my game, to get back my confidence.

The instructors split the dozens of Wildcat wannabes into teams of five. I was given the task of writing the names of my four teammates on a sheet of paper and turning in the roster. I scribbled down the forgettable names of the three other guys. Rounding out the roster was the camper I wanted.

"What's your name?" I asked.

"Anfernee Hardaway," the fifteen-year-old said.

What the hell kind of name is that? I thought.

"I don't think I can pronounce that," I responded. "You got a nickname, like Anfy or something?"

With a touch of southern politeness, he smiled. Most likely he'd heard that line before. He then spelled out his name: A-N-F-E-R-N-E-E.

"Oh, sorry. I can do that," I replied.

My team was set. We lacked a true big man, but I got my guy. I liked our chances.

He was also heading into his sophomore season of high school. He told me he was from Memphis and playing for Treadwell. I perked up. I had moved from Memphis two years earlier—first to coastal Alabama and then to a blue-collar town in middle Tennessee. I missed home.

Anfernee and I played together that week—two fifteen-year-olds leading a team against more seasoned upperclassmen. He averaged about 18 points a game. I had a decent camp, scoring about 14 points a game. Our team competed well, even without a true center manning the post. We won about 4 out of every 5 games. One time, we trailed by 1 as the clock wound down. Anfernee held the ball for the last shot. The seconds ticked away . . . *6, 5, 4 . . .*

He faked right at the free throw line and spun to his left, stretching his arm out with a soft touch. The opposing center emphatically swatted the ball—*Get that weak stuff outta here!* The ball squirted out to me at the top of the key. I fired a three-pointer at the buzzer. *Swish!* Anfernee raced toward me and we had one of those great triumphant sports hugs.

It was an incredible moment, one that's stuck with me ever since.

That shot earned me an invite to his dorm room. When he said pizzas showed up out of the blue, I realized then he wasn't just another camper. Coach Eddie Sutton wasn't having Meat Lover's Delight delivered to my room. Anfernee's room was just like the rest of the camper's, barren cinder-block walls with twin beds. But there was one exception: He had stacks of Air Jordans and other fresh sneakers piled nearly to the ceiling. I was like dang, I had to search every mall for my Jordans and dude's got like twenty pair.

We talked about Memphis State basketball—how Keith Lee,

William Bedford, and Baskerville Holmes tore up the Mid-South Coliseum. How much it hurt to see the Tigers lose to Villanova in the Final Four two years earlier, in 1985. Anfernee said his favorite NBA player was George "Iceman" Gervin, followed by Magic Johnson. Mine were Keith Lee, Larry Bird, and Michael Jordan.

Anfernee became a boon for the freshmen and sophomores at camp—we loved seeing him take some of the upperclassmen to school. The camp featured a slam dunk contest. We all crowded around, wanting to see how the youngest guy would compete. Anfernee awed everyone in the gym, even University of Kentucky standout Rex Chapman, with a rattling one-handed double-pump dunk.

Anfernee was there on a special invite. He had started his freshman year as a center at Treadwell High in Memphis on a team led by Elliot Perry, the most sought after guard in the nation, with lightning-quick speed and socks up to his knees and goggles on his face. Kentucky scouts lingered in the Treadwell gym, trying to entice the bespectacled senior sensation to Lexington. He was headed to play for the Wildcats, but his scholarship was given to Eddie Sutton's son, Sean. Elliot wound up with the hometown Memphis State Tigers, where he had a spectacular career before heading to the NBA.

But the play of the skinny freshman also raised the scouts' eyebrows: *Could Anfernee be the next great player out of Memphis?*

The Wildcats told one of his coaches, Michael Toney, to get him to Lexington for the summer camp. Toney revved up the engine of his Chrysler LeBaron, Anfernee's long legs stretching across the backseat, for the 422-mile journey.

Basketball is bigger than the Kentucky Derby. The Blue in the Bluegrass State might as well stand for the blue-and-white of the Kentucky Wildcats. It's the most storied program in the nation, although fans at the University of North Carolina–Chapel Hill would argue otherwise.

In Kentucky, the Cats put on a full-court press. The governor and mayor of Lexington had kids at the camp. But the two power players went out of their way to introduce themselves to Anfernee, another sign there was something different about the kid from Memphis. Let's just say, the governor didn't rush over to shake my hand. During the day, Anfernee played on my team; at night, he moved inside to play with the big boys—the Kentucky Wildcats. At just fifteen, he hung with Rex Chapman, Eric Manuel, and LeRoy Ellis. Even Kenny "Sky" Walker—picked fifth overall in the 1986 draft by the New York Knicks—stopped in to play. The Kentucky stars were off-limits to everyone else. We saw them only from afar. The closest we got to Sky Walker was when he hosted an autograph session downtown: He charged twenty bucks.

Even the nighttime games were closed to regular campers. I would sneak into the gym just to see how Anfernee competed with the nation's best college players.

Anfernee wasn't the best player at the camp. But as a budding high school sophomore, he learned he could play with anyone, even an NBA star.

The camp was a pivotal moment—Anfernee's coming-out party outside the borders of Memphis.

While I had a sense that he was a special player and was bound for bigger courts, I had no clue about what he'd lived through to get to this point.

We were two kids from very different sides of Memphis—a symbol of how the game of basketball bridged the divide of the racially charged city we called home. It was odd but fitting, I guess, that we met more than four hundred miles from Memphis. Anfernee and I grew up just three miles apart. But there might as well have been a concrete barrier topped with razor wire along Walnut Grove, one of the main streets running east and west, to keep us separated.

Memphis was like that in the decade following the assassination of Martin Luther King Jr. on April 4, 1968, at the Lorraine Motel downtown.

The assassination tore the city apart, and, it seems clear in retrospect, made Memphis a sort of social laboratory. While the actual signs of segregation were gone and the "Colored" water fountains were removed, the city and its citizens had much to work out.

King's assassination was a catalyst for whites to migrate to the suburbs. The gunshot was heard in every Piggly Wiggly, in every church, in every school. Whites abandoned the public school system and formed one of the most intricate private school systems in the nation in what became East Memphis. Many private schools were founded before 1968, but with the assassination and the integration of the public schools, whites—even working-class families—figured out ways to fork out thousands for tuition.

In his "I Have a Dream" speech on the steps of the Lincoln Memorial, King said he hoped "the sons of former slaves and the sons of former slave owners will be able to sit together at the table of brotherhood." But in Memphis, for the first generation of kids growing up after the killing of the civil rights icon, there was a complete and utter separation of races—not by law, but by design. We never interacted, never spoke. The main thoroughfare, Poplar Avenue, kept stretching eastward, making suburban homebuilders rich men. The neighborhoods weren't ritzy; mostly it was a bunch of cheesy *Brady Bunch* ranch homes. But there were no blacks.

From 1970 to 1980, nearly 50,000 whites fled the city center—an abandonment that changed the city from nearly 61 percent white to 51 percent white, in just ten years. And they kept running. By 2010, the city was 63 percent black; whites made up just

29 percent. Today, one in four people in the city live below poverty. The eight-county metro area ranks as the most impoverished in the nation.

Memphis always was divided. There was a reason King came to the city in April 1968 to defend workers' rights—because the city power players didn't think blacks deserved equal pay. The city on the bluff overlooking the mighty Mississippi River had flourished on the cotton trade—and those roots were firmly planted like a southern oak. The city's burgeoning black population had fled the cotton plantations of Mississippi, Arkansas, and Tennessee. As the black community grew, blues, jazz, the strains of soul music resonated from Beale Street, down Main Street, across Union Avenue, and beyond. Slow-cooked ribs and pulled-pork sandwiches, topped with cole slaw, became culinary treasures.

I lived in a completely separate world in East Memphis. It was a strange existence—one that felt like we were guinea pigs in an experiment gone wrong. It was impossible not to notice, even as a boy. In the entire history of our country, I fit into that rare group of southerners—the first generation to be born without the law of segregation. Yet there were unwritten rules that everyone understood, but few ever talked about.

"We wanted our city to come to grips with the obvious fact that it is a biracial community that needs to deal with that reality," the *Memphis Press-Scimitar* declared in its final edition on October 31, 1983. "We began that fight when the horror of lynching was still, if not in fashion, at least tolerated. We wanted our city to believe that its future lies basically in a good, viable public education system."

The city's white population didn't.

Segregation might have ended, but racism hadn't. Not by a long shot.

At Memphis University School, where preppy sons of cotton brokers, real estate developers, and doctors went to be trained for the Ivy League, the student body often erupted with a vile chant when their teams began losing to black schools: "That's all right! That's okay! You're gonna work for us one day!" Whites mocked the MATA bus system—*Moving Africans Through America*! And one of the few public high schools that had a diverse student body in the early 1980s, White Station, was dubbed "Black Station" by the white kids of East Memphis.

I grew up in Memphis in the 1970s and early 1980s. I benefited from a free private school education because my father was a headmaster of a church school, Christ Methodist Day School. I played basketball and baseball in the leagues for white kids at the same time that Anfernee learned his game at the Lester Community Center in the projects of Binghampton, a blighted neighborhood a few minutes from my own.

But on their courts, it was a much different game. Not to sound too much like a preacher, but it was a game of life. Miss a shot and hustlers were out hundreds of dollars, and you'd have to pay the price. Drive to the lane and be prepared to have your face bashed in. Talk too much trash and get your ass whupped when you're walking into the dark of night. In my basketball leagues, moms rushed to the sidelines with sliced oranges as soon as the buzzer sounded. Our dads were the coaches, constantly pushing us, telling us to do our best. Serving as our mentors. If our team got whomped, the only thing we feared after games was Mrs. Whitmire's congealed green Jell-O salad at Fellowship Hall.

The very first time I ever interacted with a black kid was in fifth grade. My baseball team swept the title in our very white league and advanced to the city playoffs, where we played an all black team. They chanted in rhythm from their dugout, swaying and clapping in unison. "Rope it in the morning, rope it in the evening. Rope! Rope!" they chanted. It was a song they sang because they were hitting the ball with such ease it was as if the ball was on a rope and they were hammering it. They annihilated us, 22–1. The next two years, we repeated as league champs; we skipped the city playoffs.

The first time I played on the same team with blacks was sixth-grade YMCA football. I don't remember conversations with my teammates. As a kid, I didn't much notice. I was too busy trying to avoid getting my face smashed in by guys twice my size. But Memphis kids, no matter what background, who didn't play sports could've gone their whole lives without encountering someone of another race. And this was a city of 600,000 with a nearly fifty-fifty breakdown between whites and blacks.

One of the few places where whites and blacks mixed was the Mid-South Coliseum, an arena that looked like the moon had fallen from the sky and been planted on earth. On game night, 11,200 whites and blacks jammed the arena for Memphis State basketball. It was here where Tiger basketball players, nearly all of them black, took center stage.

My personal love of Memphis hoops was forged during the 1980s, when the Tigers developed one of the best teams in the nation (although the wins would later be forfeited due to a slew of NCAA violations). I even tried to mimic Keith Lee's giant afro by rubbing my mom's mousse in my hair and replicating his most recent games.

It was tradition after Tiger games for kids to line up on the court and grab sweatbands off players' wrists. The most prized possessions in my room were the sweatbands of Dwight Boyd and William Bedford; they went unwashed for years on my shelf. My own coaches wouldn't have dared touch the sweatbands, a reflection of the time and era they were raised. Larry Finch, who later became the winningest coach in the history of Memphis State (now the University of Memphis), brought the city together across racial lines, for a brief moment, in 1973 when he led the Tigers to their first national title game, only to be overpowered by UCLA's Bill Walton in one of the most epic individual performances in NCAA tournament history. And the same can be said in the decades since, with the Tigers becoming the rallying cry for the city's disparate white and black population. From the era of All-American forward Keith Lee in the 1980s to coach John Calipari's reign in the 2000s, Memphians have bled Tiger blue.

After my week at Eddie Sutton basketball camp, I returned to Gallatin, a town of roughly twenty thousand people about twenty-five miles northeast of Nashville, where I played basketball at the public school. We had moved from the all-white area of East Memphis in 1984 because my father got a job with a small school in Gallatin. My brother attended college in Memphis, though, and would fill me in with reports of Anfernee's latest feats—like an alley-oop to himself where he threw the ball off the backboard and nearly tore the rim off. Another time, he won the jump ball at tip-off and three seconds later he already had his first dunk of the game. Even as he rose to become *Parade* magazine's top high school player in the nation, Memphis showed its true colors and I would often hear people making fun of his name and even his mom for choosing it.

Anfernee doesn't take offense to that now. He even laughs about it. He was told by his mom that the name stems from one of her classmates at Lester. "That's what was told to me, but I don't know, bro. Where is this dude, Anfernee? I want to meet him," Penny said to me jokingly.

I had never set foot in Binghampton, the very rough and dangerous subsidized-housing community Anfernee was from (that is, the Hood), as a kid. It was one of two places whites were told to stay away from—the other being Orange Mound, one of the first neighborhoods in America built by and for blacks, developed on what was once a plantation. The name Orange Mound stems from a hedge of osage oranges—best known in the South as horse apples—that lined the old plantation. The neighborhood, originally with 982 shotgun shacks that sold for less than a hundred bucks, bordered a KKK stronghold. Orange Mound became a hub of activity for the city's blacks. But by the 1980s, the crack epidemic decimated both Orange Mound and Binghampton.

After thirty years of being away, I came back home for a story. I had been sent by CNN to visit Binghampton for the first time, to write about Anfernee "Penny" Hardaway's having reportedly taken over coaching middle school duties for the Lester Lions. He had accepted the job as a favor to help his boyhood friend Desmond Merriweather, who was battling stage 4 cancer and could no longer commit to full-time coach.

Desmond's and my paths had actually once crossed on the court, too. A summer after I met Penny, I guarded Desmond at a basketball camp at Middle Tennessee State University. A lefty with a quick first step and a nasty three-point shot, he lit me up for about 20 points.

It was a very surreal experience for me to be back in Memphis and yet to feel like a complete stranger. Binghampton was once separated from white Memphis by a railroad track, like so many areas of the South. Just across the tracks was a nicer area, bearing the same name but without the *p*, Binghamton. Whites could sip gin and tonics and dine on well-marbled ribeyes at the nearby Memphis Country Club while turning a blind eye to the existence of Binghampton, where the city's poorest residents were crammed into a few square miles. As the years passed, the environment grew even more toxic. The crimes became black on black. Gangs ruled Binghampton—and still hold sway.

In Binghampton, the Lester Middle School and Lester Community Center anchor the neighborhood. Both facilities provide a ray of hope from the street life, as Crips, Bloods, Vice Lords, and Gangster Disciples stake their turf all around. Lester is a classic brick building that dates back to the days of segregation. There's also a five-acre park and four outdoor basketball courts where the city's best hone their skills. Along with fifties-style ranch homes and shotgun shacks, post–World War II homes with wood siding and front porches, made for telling tall tales and sipping sweet tea, surround the school. At the southern edge, two projects stand as a vestige of the past: Tillman Cove is a cluster of duplexes with broken windows where GDs and Vice Lords man the corners, their gang colors for all to see. Red Oak is a collection of Section 8 apartments where dozens of people, all living in poverty, crowd into a single apartment. Drugs are sold openly with turf constantly being scratched out by the Crips and Bloods. An empty guard gate welcomes visitors at Red Oak with a sign that says: "Notice to visitors, all persons entering this property should proceed directly to resident's unit." It's so dangerous, the sign should read: "Notice to visitors: RUN WHILE YOU CAN!"

One might expect the middle school and the community center to be covered in graffiti. Yet there is none. Residents, even the most dangerous thugs, know the buildings are hallowed ground. A mural spanning the front of the community center depicts three girls holding hands while a father looks on smiling. The sun beams down on everyone. Another mural greets visitors with an image of whites and blacks playing basketball together on the same team— a good message, to be sure, but in Memphis it's still far from reality.

Penny's story is America in a microcosm, a lesson as to how basketball is an important example in bridging the racial divide, an example of one's determination to succeed. To overcome. When we snarfed up Domino's pizza in his dorm room in Kentucky all those years before, I had no clue of the squalor in which he dwelled at 201 Red Oak in Binghampton, nor did I know our paths would cross again.

Beyond basketball, Penny has remained active in retirement. He still maintains his contract with Nike, raking in hundreds of thousands of dollars a year. He is the only retired NBA player, besides Michael Jordan, to maintain a shoe line with Nike. Some of his Foamposite shoes fetch two thousand dollars. He's a business partner in a barbershop in downtown Memphis and a turf business in Miami. He also participates in charity golf events around the country and provides commentary for NBA games.

Penny made more than $200 million playing ball and from endorsements—rising to become one of the wealthiest men in Memphis history. He doesn't need to do anything—let alone set foot in Binghampton again. Here is a guy who could so easily have turned his back on the neighborhood. Yet Binghampton needs him: It's exactly where he needs to be.

CHAPTER 2

Millions to a Penny

The brick struck Louise's pregnant belly, and she fell to the ground. The car with three white men sped off. She didn't have time to react. She and her boys were picking flowers, not too far from Zion Cemetery, just along Highway 18 in the delta flats outside Blytheville, Arkansas. She was five months pregnant with her third child.

It was the summer of 1943, when whites terrorized blacks in the rural South, when killings and lynchings and beatings of blacks were rarely investigated, rarely prosecuted. They were roundly ignored.

Pain rocketed through her womb. Louise thought she would die in the parched grass along the highway's shoulder. She lay bleeding and crying, not knowing if her baby would live or die. Between her tears, though, she found resolve. "Naw, hell, naw," she said, as she rose to her feet.

When she told her husband, Sylvester, nicknamed Big Daddy, what had happened, he ran out of the family's shotgun shack and pounded his fists into the trunk of a tree until they bled raw. The baby girl, however, would be born healthy a few months later. Louise chose the name Gloria, as in glory be to God the child survived. She'd have one more child, Fae.

Louise and Sylvester Hardaway worked in the cotton fields—
along with their children—for seven more years as sharecroppers.
Many nights during harvest were spent dipping their hands in tur-
pentine to try to find relief from ten, twelve, fourteen hours of
picking cotton, from sunup to sundown. They longed for a life away
from the cotton fields.

They eventually struck out for Memphis, seventy miles to the
south, just before the next planting season to avoid another year of
servitude. They settled in Binghampton, a black section of Memphis, on New Year's Day in 1950. Sylvester and Louise put $365
down on a small house at 2977 Forrest Avenue, a street named
after Confederate general Nathan Bedford Forrest, credited with
being the first grand wizard of the KKK—and forever immortalized in Memphis with a city park, complete with a giant statue of
him on horseback.

The walls in the Hardaway home consisted of tar paper. The
toilet was a hole in the floor. The tiny house, with three rooms and
a front porch, wasn't much but it still beat the shack and the hell
of picking cotton in the Arkansas delta.

Sylvester would soon leave, in 1956, but Louise managed to
keep the family going by working as a nanny and maid for white
families and eventually as a cook in the Memphis school system.
She reared her four children, fifteen grandchildren, and more
than a dozen cousins. Then, in 1976, when Louise was due for a
well-earned break from child-rearing, her youngest grown daughter, Fae, announced that she was going on the road to follow her
dream of being a singer. And she was taking her five-year-old son,
Anfernee, along with her.

That same *Naw, hell, naw* was Louise's argument-ending response. She wasn't going to stand in the way of her daughter's

dreams, but with Anfernee's father already out of his life, living somewhere in Chicago, she wasn't about to have him lose even more of his family.

Raising another boy wasn't what Louise had planned, yet she saw it as her duty. It was a lesson the boy would never forget: that you don't give up on a child. "She took me in right as she was retiring," he recounted years later. "She had worked her butt off all these years, had her home paid off and now was about to get a chance to relax. And then, I get dumped in her lap when I was five years old."

A strict disciplinarian, Louise demanded excellence. She wasn't going to have her grandson fall prey to neighborhood gangs. She taught him to love the Lord, to rise up when others failed. She coined the nickname Penny, because he was pretty as one. (She first called him "pretty," but in her thick southern accent it morphed over the years into Penny.)

He said she would tell him about the struggle of the cotton fields and for him to never forget. "The work was forced upon her, but it did teach her how to fend for herself and how to not depend on anybody else. And that carried over. It scarred her in a lot of ways, but it also taught her how to work hard."

His grandmother made certain her grandson feared making bad choices. "Anything I did wrong she would punish me for it, physically. Like we got whippings. We didn't get time-outs," Penny said. "When you did something wrong, here comes an extension cord, here comes a belt. You paid for it. So it made you afraid to do anything wrong, and she ruled with an iron fist. She was trying to inflict pain on me to make me afraid of doing anything wrong—and it worked.

"Most people would say that's abuse, but it's really not to me.

The old school would beat you for doing wrong, and you'd clean up your act and be afraid to do that again."

Lester Middle School, along with the Lester Community Center, served as a sanctuary away from the rest of the neighborhood's troubles. Penny could escape inside to the gym or play on one of the four outdoor basketball courts. Beyond the courts, though, pot and crack were sold in open view in adjacent Howze Park. Sirens and gunshots were part of the sound track of the neighborhood. Once a man with a sawed-off shotgun holed up in the park and opened fire on SWAT members who surrounded him. Another time, a man sprinted across the park as a car gave pursuit, a gunman spraying the hapless soul with bullets in plain sight of everyone on the basketball courts.

"That's just what you see in the neighborhood," Penny recalled. "You see murders, you see prostitution, you see gambling, you see alcohol abuse, you see drug abuse. You see the gangs. You see all that. You become numb to things that most people would go, 'Oh my God.' There's no more 'Oh my Gods' in Binghampton. You're just like, 'That's messed up.' That's really all you can say. It's just the hardship of the neighborhood that brings you to tears or brings you to doing stupid things."

Every night as darkness approached, though, Louise Hardaway's voice rang out across the neighborhood. Her call for her grandson stretched from Forrest Avenue down Tillman Street to Poplar Avenue.

"PENNNNNNNNNNNNNNNNNNNNNNNNNNNY!!!"

It didn't matter where the boy was. He'd dart home with his basketball. She'd be standing on the front porch, keeping prowl until Penny got home. It was painful as a boy to come inside when most everyone else stayed out. But Louise knew that nothing good happened after nightfall.

The outdoor courts of Lester Community Center, where Penny learned his game, are still where neighborhood hustlers gather to place bets on half-court shots. The courts also offer a refuge from the gang warfare.

"I'd be standing at the door watching my friends play. I'd sit down and cry and I thought, 'I hate this.' She said, 'When you grow up, you'll thank me for this.' Now, I'm thankful she kept me in the house. I probably could have started drinking or smoking like a lot of those kids," Penny told the *Commercial Appeal* when he was eighteen. "I've never taken a drink. I've never smoked. Every time I see a kid with drugs, I say, 'That could have been me.' Every time I see my grandmother, I thank her."

In Binghampton, the stories of the Duck are shared like the southern equivalent of Greek mythology, an untouchable Basketball God who ruled the Lester courts like Zeus. The tales so wild, so extraordinary, so legendary they're like a hand-stitched quilt, well spun and beautiful. Any hopeful basketball player who came along in Binghampton from the 1980s to early 1990s had to go through one man, Mitchell Stephenson, nicknamed the Memphis Duck. He never made it to the big leagues, but he was considered the Michael Jordan of the neighborhood. At that time, Memphis was a bastion of basketball. Everyone in the city liked to brag that Memphis produced more Division I basketball players per capita than anywhere else in the country. Future NBA first-rounders Keith Lee and William Bedford starred at Memphis State; Todd Day played at the University of Arkansas; Tony Lewis shined at the University of Alabama–Birmingham; and Baskerville Holmes, Andre Turner, Dwight Boyd, and Elliot Perry all went on to play at Memphis State and in the pros.

But the best player was the Duck.

Dude would shout: I'm gonna shit pecans before I'm gonna lose to you. And he'd clean your ass out.

He would say, Everybody look out—off the glass, you know what it is. Cash!

The Duck wore ten, twelve, fourteen pairs of socks on each foot. Like for real.

On one of my first trips to Binghampton I went on a Duck hunt. I had to find the maniacal 5-foot-8 guard with a 44-inch vertical leap whom everyone talked about. What tales might he have of the young Penny?

At a house party at the boyhood home of Anthony Douglas, the big-bodied power forward who played with Penny at Memphis State, I chowed down on slow-cooked Memphis ribs and baked beans. Anthony's mom served up her homemade caramel cake. With a wink, she confided that her secret ingredient was love. "We're so poor love is all we got to give in Binghampton," she said.

I snarfed about ten thousand calories of pure love in about ten minutes and chased it with beer. A Miller Lite in hand, I walked down the driveway and to the quiet cul-de-sac, one of the few areas of Binghampton where it seems nearly everyone on the street remains married.

That's when I saw the Duck. He was hunched over the bed of his red pickup truck. He stuck out his tough leathery hand and introduced himself. "I can tell you about everything that done come down through here," he said, his voice muffled as if he had a mouthful of tobacco.

"They call me the Legend. Mitchell Stephenson, the Duck. I didn't make pro, but my voice speaks for itself. I can stop a riot before it even starts. I had a game you ain't never seen. I was the Michael Jordan. I was goooooood, man."

Every time he said the word *man*, it sounded more like the strain of a guitar on Beale Street: maaaaaaaainnnnnnnn. I mean, when the Duck talked, he resembled a mallard in the lobby of the Peabody Hotel, strutting around, his barrel chest swelled, his pride on full display. Binghampton was his penthouse.

The stories flowed slow and sweet with an extra bite like Tennesse whiskey. Before he continued, I had to know about his socks. "People say you wore like ten pair on each leg."

He leaned so close I could see his sweaty pores. The deal with the socks, he told me, was that he kept twisting his ankles as a teen in the early 1970s and needed better ankle support. "One day I come home, my momma had put all my brother's socks together. I said, 'Here's what I'm gonna do. I'm gonna put all these mothas on.' I put twenty on each leg. I had forty socks total.

"That's right. I wore forty pairs of socks. When it came time to play, if one of those socks was missing, I could tell you. And in football, they called me the Mummy. Everything I had on I had two sets of everything. Only thing I didn't have two sets of was the helmet. It would take me an hour and a half to get dressed."

I tried to envision the young basketball version of the Duck—a squatty guy with twenty socks on each leg, dunking on everybody.

The Duck graduated from East High School in 1973, the first integrated class at the once-heralded all-white public school. "It was kinda rough, but we worked through it." He wouldn't elaborate on whatever bad stuff he encountered there.

"If I could do it again, I'd go back," he said. "One thing about it is we all gotta live when we're done talking. You see what I'm saying, Bossman. It don't matter if he's green, white, or black—if he's a good person, he's good. You gotta respect that."

His is another cautionary tale of what might have been. A prospective All-American in basketball and football during high school, he blew his chance to make it out of the neighborhood. He'd been recruited to play basketball by Memphis State, but in his senior season against the elite Memphis University private school, he fouled out late in the game—and flipped out cussing at the refs. Memphis State withdrew the scholarship. The University of Nebraska recruited him for football, but he didn't have the grades. He went to a junior college in Arizona but he had other things on his mind.

"You went out there and got laid, didn't you," I said.

His guffaw confirmed my suspicions.

The Duck returned to Binghampton, worked at the Lester Community Center for fifteen years, and got a job as a sanitation employee with the city. He mentored every high school All-American who emerged from Binghampton: Anthony Douglas, Billy Smith, Sylvester Gray, Elliot Perry, Penny.

"I treated them all like family," he said.

He paused. "I found out everybody don't make pro. Some people do, some people don't. That's what the kids have got to learn."

The Duck's quack got even more animated when he moved to telling favorite Penny stories.

"Awwwww, Penny was something you ain't never seen. Dude growed overnight. He was beautiful," Duck said.

"I was the best in the Hood. Every Sunday morning, he'd come get me. He'd say, 'Let's play one-on-one.' He'd say, 'I ain't gonna be good till I beat you, Duck.' Man, that dude got good. But looka here, I beat him all the time. When he got good, I ain't beat him no more. Awww, it was so beautiful, man. I could've kissed him he was so beautiful."

I wanted more, for the Duck to give me the lowdown on the first time Penny turned the table. It was the summer of 1987. Penny had just returned from Eddie Sutton basketball camp in Kentucky. "It was a Sunday morning. Dude had the ball in his hand. He said, 'Duck, I'm ready.'

"I said, 'How can you be ready? Come on, fool, let's go.'

"He said, 'I'm gonna beat you.'

"I said, 'Man, you can't beat me, Dog.'

"We got up there to Lester and he beat me. Then, he come back the next week and got me again. I thought it was a fluke the first time, but dude came back and got me. You know what I told him, 'Boy, you're on your game now. You're fixing to roll. You're fixing to end up in the NBA.'"

Was it embarrassing to lose to a fifteen-year-old? I asked.

"I liked it, because I knowed he had grown up. If you can beat me, you're supposed to be the next person, the next legend. . . . When he beat me, he respected me for it. He said, 'I liked that, Dog. Good game.' He was just a good kid. He made you want to be on his team. He wasn't a hater."

As I spoke with Duck, Big Slaw Dog, the black equivalent of the

Incredible Hulk, joined in. A long-feared neighborhood enforcer turned Penny bodyguard, Big Slaw Dog added relish and mustard to these yarns. Standing at 6-1 and 275 pounds of sheer muscle, he had enough gold teeth to supply Fort Knox.

I asked exactly how good Duck was back in the day.

"Shiiiiiiiiiiiiiiiiiiiiit, man. Come on," said Big Slaw Dog, whose real name is James Malone. "Man would run fifteen in a row. He'd say, 'I'm fixing to hit every fifteen one of these and then we going out the door.' Tell me he wouldn't say that. He'd fall in the corner. Foop. Shiiiiiiiiiiiiiiiiiiit! Cold, man, cold."

Penny's cousin LaMarcus Golden later told me that "beating the Memphis Duck would be the equivalent of a kid beating LeBron James or Kobe Bryant. No one could beat him or outplay him. When Penny beat Duck, if you didn't see it, you heard about it. Word spread through Binghampton like crazy."

If I wanted an even better picture of the young Penny, I was told to meet Antoine Richardson, a neighborhood hustler who gave Penny a basketball when he was five. Antoine lived across the road from Penny's grandma on Forrest Avenue and pitched in with raising him. Antoine once served five years in prison for selling marijuana—a symbol of how closely intertwined everyone is in Binghampton, how such giant swings of good and evil lurk on a single road.

When Antoine got released from prison, he found a new calling: mentoring the neighborhood ballplayers and trying to steer them away from a life of crime. Like the Duck, Antoine can tell a story. When he got on a roll, he licked his lips and paused when he felt others nearby were getting too loud. "Looka here," he said, "a man's trying to tell a story to this fine gentleman. Y'all need to move on and hush down."

Then he started up like an old-school Cadillac, a slow purr that led to a pedal-to-the-metal pace.

"Penny came out of the womb a born shooter," said Antoine. He danced his hips, pretended to put on a shake-and-bake move to illustrate Penny's soft shooting touch.

"I didn't know how tall he was gonna get, but that boy could shoot the ball. I made him play a boy named Cricket Lighter every day. Penny would always win the first game. They'd play two out of three. Penny wouldn't never let him win that third game."

The Memphis Duck, Big Slaw Dog, the Cricket Lighter—I couldn't help but think how much I loved this place.

"That boy Penny used to come up every day with some game. He kept that ball in his hand. I'd say, 'Penny, one thing I like about you is you can shoot. A lot of folks like to dribble and act like a fool but you can put the ball in the hole. I like that about you, boy!' As time went on, Penny stayed humble. A lot of us got into a lot of trouble. He didn't never go to jail. Penny was a great human being coming up. He's genuine. You can see that in him right now, and I love that about him."

Antoine was among the first to call him Lil Penny, a lanky kid with long arms and a touch of southern gentleman. Penny always sprinkled his answers with "yes, sir."

"Just a polite kid," he said. "There was a lot of stuff Penny had going against him, but by him having a praying grandmother, she kept him out of all that. His grandmomma is the reason he's where he's at today. Just a beautiful woman with a heart of gold."

While living with his grandmother, Penny heard from his mother sporadically, mostly from postcards she sent from the road: California, Alaska, and Hawaii. Penny met his dad only once in his early years. His father came in from Chicago, demanding the boy return with him, saying he was entitled to raise his son. Never one to back down, Louise got in his face and screamed about how he'd never changed a diaper, never tended the boy's wounds, never even shared a hug with the boy.

Not too many people ever won an argument with Louise. Penny's father went back to Chicago, without his son.

Penny closed ranks at an early age, keeping guard on who to let in on his life, but he had two great friends: LaMarcus Golden and Desmond Merriweather, two years his younger. They would play basketball every day on the courts outside Lester Middle School or inside the gym at the community center.

But when you're a rising basketball star it is easy to get caught up in your own hype, and Penny was not immune. While Duck and Antoine Richardson tried to counsel him when they could, they were never going to be a substitute for a father. And there were others in the neighborhood who had less than altruistic intentions. They saw dollar signs for themselves, a way out of the Hood if they latched on. And then there is the problem of just being fifteen. In the Treadwell High gym on game nights, girls with purposeful low tops and short skirts would compete for his attention. Drug dealers with trench coats, their guns tucked inside, sat next to scouts in pressed polo shirts from Kentucky, Tennessee, Georgetown, Memphis State, and Arkansas.

"So much is glorified in Memphis, especially in basketball," said LaMarcus Golden, who was also a teammate at Treadwell. "You're put on a pedestal real quick and so many people look up to you when you're a superstar, there are so much temptations: you have girls, you have drugs, you have gangs. Once you become a superstar, it can be middle school, high school, college: People have the sense to gravitate toward you because you're getting so much attention. . . . There's just so much that comes along with it. And there's so many broken homes and broken families in the city, we don't have the right leadership a lot of times. We don't have the right guidance. We need people to tell us what's right and help us through certain situations. If you don't have the right guidance, you can easily be led the wrong way and make the wrong choices and go down the wrong path."

Penny's main guidance counselor was his gritty grandma.

One of those who sought Penny was Nolan Richardson, the head coach of the University of Arkansas. Richardson scored a coup when he persuaded Todd Day, then the best player in Memphis, to come to Arkansas. He hoped Penny would do the same, the perfect fit for what would become known as his 40 Minutes of Hell program. "You've got the complete package of Larry Bird, Magic Johnson, and Michael Jordan," Richardson once told me. "Anfernee can do it all."

But Louise Hardaway, thinking back to her own hell in Arkansas, was quick with the *Naw, hell, naw.*

Penny's mother also returned to Binghampton, when Penny was about fifteen. Her music career had run its course. He moved out of his grandmother's house and into apartment 201 in the Red Oak projects with his mother. The two later moved across the road to #7 duplex in Tillman Cove, an equally dangerous project where Anfernee slept on a twin bed with his skinny legs hanging over the end, touching the floor. The move was a rough transition—drug deals and shootings all around. He missed his grandmother and their daily conversations on the front porch. He tried to see her as often as he could. He filled that void by playing ball as much as he could.

"It was very difficult, because my mom was all over the place," Penny said. "Even though I moved back in with my mom, it was much easier to get into trouble. My grandmother was very strict; my mom was waaaay more lenient. So I could've gotten into a lot more trouble, but what my grandmother instilled in me stayed with me. So I didn't really do anything out of the norm."

His mother became a fixture at his games, but even after Penny rose to become the top-ranked high school basketball player in the nation his dad never saw him play.

"I met my dad when I was six or seven, then he left," Penny told me. "From when I was age five until eighteen, I had only seen him maybe three or four times. He wasn't present in my life.

"I really never saw him, but it never really bothered me. I mean, I would wonder every now and then, as any kid would, what my father was doing, wishing my father was here. But I would snap out of it really quickly and just keep doing what I needed to do."

Yet the same thing that ended the Duck's career and many others—the lack of discipline—threatened to end Penny's. Tennessee's governing sports body, TSSAA, in the late 1980s instituted a "No Pass, No Play" policy. For athletes across the state, it was a rule they thought could be ignored: Coaches had always talked of sitting players out if they failed classes, but they rarely did. They might've sat players out for a quarter or two, but come clutch time the stars were always inserted back in games. But this time the rule was mandatory. Coaches and players were powerless once a teacher submitted the grades. Pleading forgiveness to a coach or teacher did no good. Penny would learn this lesson the hard way.

The summer before his senior high school season, Penny was invited to attend the elite Nike/ABCD basketball camp at Princeton University, where 128 of the nation's top high schoolers gathered for a week of basketball and academics. Nike formed the camp because it realized that many black basketball players, especially those from the nation's inner cities, struggled to read at grade level and weren't prepared for the SAT and ACT to get into college. It was also a good opportunity for Nike to get in the good graces of future NBA players. Forty percent of those at the camp tested below grade level; one in ten were functionally illiterate. Of the top six players of the 1990 class, three would be forced to sit out their freshman seasons in college, academically ineligible players known as Prop 48s. Penny would be one of those.

At the camp in Princeton, Penny met Spike Lee, whose movie *Do the Right Thing* had just hit theaters. He cautioned the players to look beyond basketball.

That theme was repeated throughout the week. There were more tutorials and lectures than basketball at the camp. Eleven high school teachers tried to improve the players' reading skills and quizzed them in SAT prep sessions. In the evening the camp provided counselors who offered guidance on how to handle the pressures of being top recruits and being sought by every media member in the nation. The players were mostly eighteen, with spotty academic training and about to be thrust onto a national stage where millions could be made off them.

Frank DuBois, the camp's academic director, said he understood it might be too late to intervene. The boys were already set in their ways and a week was insufficient to make headway with them academically because they were so far behind. The teens needed intervention at a much earlier age. They should've gotten help years before, at the middle school level, for any real academic improvement. But DuBois told the *Chicago Tribune* that "if we just reach two kids," then the camp will have succeeded.

It would take years to reach its full effect on Penny.

But at the time, those instructions went to the wayside. Penny stopped attending many of his classes at Treadwell at the start of his senior year. His algebra teacher failed him, forcing him to miss much of his senior season. At a house party, a known drug dealer looked at him and said, "Oh, you're the dumb ballplayer." At one basketball camp, Duke coach Mike Krzyzewski walked by without saying a word. The young Penny believed it was an intentional snub, a coach of an elite school unwilling to acknowledge the existence of someone from the Hood.

Skipping classes proved costly. It robbed Penny of becoming the most prolific high school scorer in Memphis history—and even though he joined the team midseason, Treadwell fell short of its goal of winning the state championship. Penny averaged 34 points, 8 rebounds, 7 assists, and 3 steals that season—in which, if he had played its entirety, he would've easily set the city scoring record. He tried five times to pass the ACT and fell just short every time. The failure made him miss his freshman season at Memphis State because of academic ineligibility.

"I deserved to be failed because I wasn't going to class," he said. "It wasn't that I couldn't do the work. I started really believing the hype and wasn't going to school. So I learned my lesson from that. . . . But it helped me more than it hurt me. I knew that I wanted basketball in my life and that education was going to be a part of it. It made me start doing my work, and I started going to school."

At Memphis State, Tim Sumner headed the university's academic service program for athletes. Memphis State had a terrible record of graduating basketball players. During one stretch from 1975 to 1985, not a single black player—out of a couple dozen—graduated.

Sumner made it his mission to get Penny up to eligibility levels. Sumner was under a great deal of pressure himself from the media, the school, and the city to get Penny to study. He told the *Memphis Business Journal* that it was appalling "this city would put so much importance on the future basketball career of a 17-year-old."

"The intensity of that attention could have done nothing but put more pressure on him," Sumner said. "But the young man now has the opportunity to make it or break it on his own. If he has the desire, I have the utmost confidence he can make it."

Penny's first collegiate game was a coronation fit for a king. He had missed his freshman year due to academic woes. He hadn't played competitively for a year and a half and he'd even survived a shooting during that time, in which the bullet ricocheted off the pavement and lodged in his foot. Memphis breathed a sigh of relief that he survived, relatively unscathed, and now was finally suited up to play for the hometown Tigers.

It was the grand opening of the Las Vegas–worthy Great American Pyramid, a twenty-thousand-seat arena that nearly doubled the size of Memphis State's previous home. The sixth largest pyramid in the world glistened in the night, shimmering along the Mississippi River. It was built with huge fanfare, a tourist destination meant to revive a desolate downtown. Basketball fans liked to joke, though, that it was built to thank the best basketball player in Memphis history for staying home to play college ball, for rejecting powerhouse programs at Kentucky and Arkansas.

The lights dimmed. The 20,142 fans rose to their feet. The spotlight zoomed in on No. 25.

"*Anfernee Hardaway!*" the voice boomed over the PA system.

The Tigers were playing the inaugural game of the Great Midwest conference against rival DePaul University.

The game was nip-and-tuck. But DePaul was spoiling the city's perfect script. With time winding down, the Tigers trailed, 77–74. The skinny Penny brought the ball up court. The whole city awaited this moment: the local legend with the game on the line.

. . . 10, 9, 8, 7 . . .

Penny let fly a three-pointer from so deep it seemed like he was standing across town at Elvis's home, Graceland. "The legend has just been born," Jim "Jimmy V" Valvano, the great college coach turned ESPN broadcaster, screamed into the microphone. "The biggest night in Memphis State basketball. The arena. The Pyramid. The place packed. And Penny Hardaway . . . what does he do? The Tomb of Doom. He bombs the *three!*"

But the celebration was short-lived. The Tigers would lose in overtime, 92–89. In the locker room, Penny slouched over. He was angry and heartbroken. He felt he'd let down the whole city. He finished with 18 points, 15 rebounds, 6 assists, and 4 steals. But the stat line he remembered most was his turnovers—13. If he had just one fewer turnover, Memphis would've won.

Despite the loss, Valvano was right: The legend had been born. Penny led the team to the Elite Eight that year, losing to conference rival Cincinnati by 31 points, the fourth time that season the Bearcats bested Memphis State. Penny was named an All-American and played on the developmental Olympic team that practiced against the 1992 Dream Team, the greatest basketball team ever made with stars like Michael Jordan, Larry Bird, and Magic Johnson suiting up. In the classroom, Penny earned his way onto the dean's list with a 3.4 GPA.

The hype went into overdrive. There are two plays that are still legendary in Memphis: In a blowout against Southwest Louisiana State, Penny got a breakaway; his teammate bounced the ball around half-court, Penny caught it on the fly and threw it down. At the Maui Invitational against Chaminade, Penny described "zigzagging this guy in and out. I went behind my back with the right hand and when it hit my left hand, I went right behind my back to the guy on the trailer and he dunked it." His junior season he averaged nearly 23 points a game, 8.5 rebounds, 6 assists, 2.4 steals, and 1.2 blocks. But the Tigers ended on a disappointing note, losing 55–52 in the first round of the NCAA tournament to the Western Kentucky Hilltoppers.

That season, agents flooded his answering machine daily and sent him letters to try to entice him away from the college ranks. Some showed up in the stands in the Pyramid. They also sent stars to do their dirty work: Spike Lee and NFL Hall of Famer Reggie White came down to Memphis. NBA scouts sat along press row, often as many as half a dozen. "It doesn't impress me that there's a superstar in our crowd who came to see me," Penny said.

Penny made the decision to leave Memphis State before his senior season to enter the draft. Draft day was in Detroit on June 30, 1993. Penny had tried out with the Orlando Magic the day before. "He was absolutely spectacular. He impressed everyone in the building and practically everyone within a half mile," said Magic president Dick DeVos. Penny and Shaquille O'Neal, the megastar center for Orlando, tore up the court. "I felt I had a great showing in Orlando. I felt really good about playing there." The scouts and management knew they had their guy. Penny sent a giant poster of himself to Magic vice president John Gabriel to try to influence the draft. "I have to admit, that was pretty original," Gabriel said.

Orlando had the No. 1 draft pick.

Penny had been told not to worry if his name wasn't selected first—"They said if you get drafted by Golden State, you're going to get traded." Chris Webber, the star of the University of Michigan Fab Five, was initially chosen by Orlando. With the No. 3 pick, Golden State chose Penny. He stood and hugged his mother and then his grandmother with her feathery gray hair. His mother wept.

"You're sitting there and you hear your name called and you're wondering, 'Wow, is that real?'" he recalled.

The twenty-one-year-old Penny put on a poker face and played the part: He wore a Golden State Warriors cap, walked across the red carpet, and shook hands with NBA commissioner David Stern. He was immediately ushered on camera with TNT reporter Craig Sager, who said trade rumors were swirling. "How much anxiety is going through you right now?"

"I came in kind of nervous, but I'm feeling pretty good right now," Penny said. "Nothing compares to this. You only get drafted once. It's a feeling of a lifetime that I'll never forget."

Sager then asked about going from failing grades in high school to the dean's list in college. "It was a hard process, but I knew that I could do it. In high school, I didn't want to do it. I never prepared myself to do my homework and all that. But once I got to college, I knew I had to. So that's when it all came to the plate. It wasn't that I couldn't; I just didn't want to. So I just made the change in college and started doing it."

Sager drew the microphone to his mouth, saying Penny was "a great example" of someone who stood for more than just basketball, a shining example that everyone could admire.

Within minutes, Stern strode to the podium. "There's been a trade," he said. Penny was going to Orlando, effectively making him the No. 1 selection of the draft. He told reporters he looked forward to playing with Shaq. "We're going to play great together as soon as he knows some of my passes," Penny said at the time. "Some of my passes may go out the door before they get to the rim, but we're going to be great once we get it down. I can't wait to get it on in the NBA."

He made another promise to his grandmother that day—that he would earn his degree, which he eventually did from Memphis State in 2003. His major was education. "Other than being draft-ed, the most satisfying feeling I've ever had was getting my college degree," he said. "Going and walking across the stage to get my diploma, I finished something that I started off doing. I left college early, but I always promised myself I'd return. And I did that in 2003. It wasn't easy, being in the NBA and trying to take online courses and traveling and going to practice. . . . That day, when I walked, will always be a special day in my life."

Penny chose two up-and-coming black sports agents, Carl and Kevin Poston, to act as his agents. Laid-back guys who preferred blue jeans over pressed suits, the Postons entered the boardroom guns a-blazing. When Penny went into the NBA, it was the Wild West of salary negotiations, with agents demanding astronomical money—and typically getting their way. The Postons made Penny hold out. They had secured a $2 million trading card deal for him and Penny made about $400,000 on the movie *Blue Chips*, a basketball movie in which he starred alongside Shaq.

The Postons postured. "Banks could borrow money from Anfernee right now," Carl Poston said as the contract talks dragged on. "The pressure is on the Magic, not us.

"Anfernee has money and major offers from Europe to play basketball there. . . . He'd rather play in Orlando, but he won't sign for anything less than his market value. He can sit tight for a while."

When reports surfaced that they rejected a $50 million offer, fans were outraged. The headline in Orlando read: "No Play, Plenty of Pay Are OK with Hardaway." He missed training camp to squeeze the Magic further. In the end, the Postons got him a $65 million deal, the second highest in sports history at the time—far higher than the legends Magic, Michael, and Larry. When Penny suited up for his first exhibition, many fans booed. The Poston brothers always downplayed those tensions: Fans were finicky; they'd turn around once Penny shined.

"I was blessed to get the contracts I had," Penny told me, "for something I would've done for free."

The kid from the projects of Memphis slept on his first king-sized bed in his five-bedroom mansion in one of Florida's most exclusive neighborhoods, Isle Worth. "All my beds up to that point were twin beds, all through high school, all through college," he said. "Think about me in a twin bed. To move from a Section 8 apartment in the Red Oak projects to a duplex in Tillman Cove where the homes are split, into a five-bedroom mansion with king-sized beds, it was an amazing feeling. I don't think I went to sleep the first night. I sat in bed with my windows open, just looking out, saying, 'Wow, I can't believe this is happening.'"

The leap to the pros came with other huge responsibilities. "It's a blessing to be able to have the money, but it's a lot tougher because you get so many people coming out of the woodwork wanting money, needing money, asking you for money." He returned home in spurts, most of the time to participate in charity events. In 1995, he raised $100,000 for Memphis charities in a game in his hometown, including $25,000 for the National Civil Rights Museum. The next year he scored 71 points in the same charity event and raised tens of thousands dollars more. Many times he'd stop and hand out money to homeless people and others who had fallen on hard times. "You get your naysayers—that I never come back to the neighborhood. I was doing everything silently. I didn't need it in the paper," Penny told me. "I've had publicists and PR people tell me you should put everything you do in the paper. Well, I'm not that guy. I don't need people praising me. I do it because God put it in my heart to do it. As long as He knows, I'm okay with it. I don't have to pump up everything I do."

In the early 1990s, the league was searching for the next great guard. Magic Johnson and Michael Jordan were entering the twilight of their careers—with Magic's brought on more suddenly when he announced he was HIV-positive. Larry Bird's days with the Boston Celtics were over. There were no obvious players coming through the college ranks who had big-time star potential at guard. And the guard spot was where the NBA built its reputation and where shoe companies made hundreds of millions of dollars.

Even with all the talent possessed by the powerhouse programs of the early 1990s—UNLV's Larry Johnson and Stacey Augmon, Michigan's Chris Webber and Jalen Rose, Duke's Christian Laettner and Bobby Hurley—none of those players made the transition to long-term stardom. Yes, they were talented enough to play in the NBA, but they weren't good enough to build entire franchises around. Let alone to stake the reputation of an entire shoe company.

Yet there was one player who kept turning the heads of shoe executives. The Jewel of the Mississippi River. The 6-foot-7 guard out of Memphis whose unique high dribbling approach was dubbed: "They reach, I teach."

Reebok was saturating the market thanks to a megadeal with Shaq. Converse was reeling because Magic and Larry—the shoe company's main moneymakers—no longer carried the same gravitas. So convinced Penny was their next big hit, Converse offered him a multiyear deal worth more than $7 million. They even had a commercial already prepared to hit TV, showing Penny playing all five positions on the court.

But Nike was the shoe he preferred. And Penny got what he wanted. He became the face of one of the most famous ad campaigns in sports history, with Spike Lee–produced commercials. In the ads, Chris Rock famously voiced "Lil Penny," the trash-talking alter ego of the humble Hardaway. "You can't guard me. The Secret Service couldn't guard me," Lil Penny once boasted.

Everything went his way. Back in Memphis, he was the face of an antidrug initiative with the Shelby County sheriff's department. Its slogan: "Be smart, stay clean, and keep the dream." He was never too far from his hometown, known around Memphis for stopping at local basketball gyms—from the rough Lester courts to the Gothic halls of Rhodes College. He loved the surprised looks of the locals when he suited up with them: "It really keeps me grounded to what's really important in life. You can only buy so many things for yourself or people around you. It's all about giving back yourself. I love that."

In just his second season, Penny helped lead the young Magic franchise to the NBA Finals in 1995. Orlando faced the defending champion Houston Rockets, an aging team powered by Hakeem Olajuwon, Clyde Drexler, and Kenny Smith. Yet the veteran Rockets swept the upstart Magic.

It would be the closest Penny would ever come to a championship season. Shaq bolted for his preferred team, the Los Angeles Lakers, the following summer and paired up with another talented guard, Kobe Bryant, then eighteen. The two built a new Lakers dynasty. Shaq announced his move to L.A. during the Summer Olympics in Atlanta, even as he and Penny helped bring home the gold for Team USA. "My first day here, which was my birthday, Shaquille signs with the Lakers. Then the bomb went off next to our hotel in Centennial Park. And then we had a bomb threat at our hotel, and we had to evacuate," Penny told the Memphis paper at the time.

With Shaq gone, the dynasty that Orlando hoped to become came to a crashing halt. Penny still dominated. He made the NBA all-star team four times, from 1995 to 1998. But the hopes and dreams of Magic fans were shattered. It worsened when Penny fell injured early in the 1997–98 season, requiring the first of what would become six knee surgeries. He never suffered the dramatic Joe Theisman grotesque injury, where the whole world watches one's agony on a never-ending loop on *SportsCenter*. Penny's injuries were nagging ones, built up over time. He got little sympathy. Angry NBA fans accused him of dogging it, a star simply collecting his paycheck and not giving it his all. The surgeon drilled a hole in his knee. It only made the pain worse. His final surgery, in 2001, was supposed to heal a microfracture, a tiny break near his left knee.

"I was a guinea pig because I didn't hear anybody else publicly having microfracture surgery," Penny told me. "I was one of the first casualties of that."

It proved devastating. "It took me a full year, almost a year and a half, before I felt normal again. I had no quad muscle anymore. That's why I couldn't jump anymore. I ran funny because there was nothing anymore to cushion that blow, of constant pounding, except for my knee. And when your knee hits, you feel that pain and you don't want to land, you don't want to push off. People didn't really know what I was going through."

For many basketball fans it felt that as soon as Penny stormed into the NBA, his career was sidelined. Even Nike downplayed the seriousness of the injuries at first: Lil Penny showed up in commercials on crutches with a bum knee. The Penny Hardaway that the basketball world had instantly come to love would never be the same. The man who had once dunk-faced Patrick Ewing, who had schooled Michael Jordan, suffered a fall from the limelight like few other superstars.

Penny remained in the league until 2007 but never regained his true form. He limped off the court after sixteen years—with the Orlando Magic, the Phoenix Suns, the New York Knicks, and the Miami Heat—with an average of 15 points, 5 assists, 4 rebounds. For many, those types of numbers mark a solid career. Yet for basketball enthusiasts—and for Hardaway himself—they represent a painful reminder of what could have been: a player with so much talent who became a casualty of the grueling eighty-two-game NBA season, who reached the top of his game only to be robbed of his full potential. Penny chooses to look at the most optimistic view: He had six great years that most anyone would die for. His grandparents began as sharecroppers; he grew up in the projects of Binghampton to become the most famous Memphian beyond Elvis—how can one complain?

"You're so young. You think it's going to happen over and over again," Penny said, of reaching the NBA championships. "You don't really get to cherish it as much, because you're thinking I'll be back next year or the year after to play for the title. But injuries happen, people leave—you don't even account for all that."

Among fans, the debate still rages: Was it his attitude that kept him back? Was he messed up by poor trades of those negotiating on his behalf? Are the doctors to blame for screwing up his knee?

Buzz Braman, Penny's longtime shooting coach, known throughout the NBA as the Shot Doctor, said it's bizarre that in a world of egomaniacs Penny "took a hit" because he was humble. Braman said there's no doubt in his mind what is to blame: the doctors. "Penny doesn't go around saying the surgeries that he had—that they misdiagnosed it. Well, I can. They misdiagnosed it. They operated on the wrong thing. And it started a spiral of, what?, five knee surgeries on one knee. You have what would have been one of the top fifty players ever, and who comes back from that?

"His first five, six years he was on his way to the Hall of Fame. If he'd had ten years uninjured, he'd be in the Hall of Fame."

Whatever the cause, Penny's career came to an unceremonious end with the Miami Heat. There was no farewell tour, no packed arenas bidding him good-bye.

Ironically, he had begun his career in a game against the Heat. In that game his rookie season, Penny scored 12 points, grabbed 8 rebounds, and dished out 8 assists—what everyone assumed was the start of the next great one. In the end, he was informed of the Heat's decision to waive him before practice in December 2007. Miami pushed Penny aside to make room for Luke Jackson, a kid who would soon be cut and playing for the lowly D-league Idaho Stampede.

The door shut on Penny's pro career at the age of thirty-six.

CHAPTER 3

The Soldier

Penny gently pushed the door open to the seventh-floor room. His instinct may have been to burst into the room and energize the crowd as he had been known to do in his playing days. But this was a hospital and this was no game.

When Desmond Merriweather saw Penny, he immediately sat up and gave his friend a smile despite his cancer-racked body reducing him to almost a skeleton and a staph infection that had weakened him further. Penny gently smothered him with a hug. It was a miracle Desmond was even alive, let alone awake and able to speak. Even the doctors had given up on him days earlier; his family had prepared for his funeral.

The expected response would have been for Desmond to let his friend know how grave the situation was looking, but instead he immediately steered the conversation to the upcoming season of Lester Middle School's basketball team, of which he was the coach. Desmond was like that: One of the few men dedicated to shaping boys into men, the right way. A few months back he had talked with Penny about getting the Lester Lions new uniforms and wanted to make sure he was still on board, with the first practice only two weeks away.

"Look, I ain't worried about no uniforms," Penny said.

The two smiled and laughed and quickly got down to one-upping each other with tall tales of their own days playing on the Lester courts. Dez spoke of the time *Sports Illustrated* came to the outdoor courts to photograph Penny. Dez and other guys from the neighborhood crowded around, taunting Penny while the photographer snapped away. Penny tried to ignore them, told them to go on and get. As they walked off, Dez and the others were in awe that one of their own had risen to become one of the most talked-about players in the nation.

In the hospital, Dez explained how much the neighborhood missed Penny. The NBA phenom had never forgotten his roots—he sent money to Lester Middle School and the Lester Community Center throughout his NBA career, always done quietly, away from the press. He'd show up for a camp for half a day during the summer and then be gone. Other times, he hopped out unannounced at Memphis courts and played with the kids. But it had been years since he'd spent quality time in his old stomping grounds. Who could blame him—his goal had always been to get out of the projects for him and his family.

Coach Desmond Merriweather standing in front of Lester Middle School.

Penny shifted the conversation. He told Dez how much he admired him—that he had always been a fighter, as a basketball player and an advocate to change the neighborhood.

"I'm still fighting," Desmond said.

Two years older than Desmond, Penny had served almost as his big brother. By blood, they were distant cousins, and the two shared many parallels in their life stories, including not having a father in their lives and their moms being absent for a chunk of their childhoods. Desmond had lived with his grandmother, too, but she died within a year of his moving in with her. "I had to look at life from a different perspective. I always wanted a dad, which I never had," Desmond recalled. "The older guys in the neighborhood—the gang members, the drug dealers, the killers, the elders—they all protected me and took me in and kept me safe from what all was going on. The street hustlers, the pimps, the killers: Those were my father figures.

"They were the people who I saw growing up, but they never did anything like that in front of me. I just knew what they did. Everybody in the neighborhood would talk about what they did. That's actually who raised me. That's what taught me my toughness."

They called him "the shining light," a radiant kid able to internalize so much and excel despite the forces working against him. His high school basketball coach nicknamed Desmond "Man Child."

Basketball became a refuge for both Penny and Desmond, a place to escape the suffocating madness of life in the Hood. While Penny would go on to star for the Memphis State Tigers and then the NBA, Desmond was his understudy, a shooting guard who hoped to follow in Penny's footsteps at Memphis State and the pros. But Desmond couldn't replicate the talent or luck that carried Penny.

Desmond was eleven when his mom left. She'd fallen in love

with a man and headed to Alexandria, Virginia. Desmond and his brother, Marty, begged to stay in Memphis. Their grandparents, Milton and Geneva Winston, agreed to raise the two boys. Discipline was foremost in the Winston home. Milton was a veteran of the Korean War and known as Daddy Buck. No one betrayed Daddy Buck. If you did, you'd have to pay with a whupping: "You'd stop what you were doing right then and get some act right in you, because he didn't play." Still on military time, Daddy Buck would awaken the grandkids at 5 A.M. every day. "If y'all want to eat breakfast, you gotta wake up at this time." He taught them at an early age that time was not to be wasted.

A devout Christian, his grandmother didn't want Desmond to go anywhere without God's help. "You better learn while you are young, because you're gonna grow up soon and you ain't gonna get no more free passes." He played basketball in white church leagues, quickly rising to become a scoring sensation—the chubby kids unable to compete with his skills and quickness. Gifts would arrive at their home—typically hams and turkeys, enough to put food on the table. His grandma would ask why all the stuff was showing up. "Grandma, I just play basketball real good," he told her.

But a year later, his safety net was rocked. While Desmond slept on the floor next to her, she awoke one night. She'd been suffering from kidney problems. "I'm not coming back no more," she told him.

The next morning, his grandmother checked into the hospital. She never returned. Desmond always loved making her proud. "When Grandma died, life became rougher," he recalled. "I wasn't getting all the valuable life lessons anymore. I was a bastard child straying away from the discipline."

With his wife gone, Daddy Buck moved out of Binghampton

and couldn't or didn't take the boys; Desmond moved in with his auntie in a dingy two-bedroom apartment with five other kids in projects across from the Lester Community Center. He slept on the floor in the living room. When thunderstorms came, the room filled with three inches of water. He'd sneak out and take quilts from a nearby storage unit and fold them into a makeshift mattress. He called it a "water bed without even asking for one." The place stunk of mold and mildew and urine.

The apartment sat next to the dangerous Red Oak projects, where twenty-five to thirty people crammed into ragtag two-bedroom apartments. He bore witness to things a kid should never have to experience, from shoot-outs to actual killings: "When we were growing up, we would see people get shot in the park. Just a whole lot of crazy chaotic things.

"That just made you want to do better, by seeing it, like I don't want to go down that road others went down. I don't want to be a casualty, a victim of circumstances."

Desmond walked to Lester Middle with his cousins, essentially serving as a young father figure. He made sure they stayed safe, and the local gangs respected him for it—they didn't try to beat his ass or initiate him by having him stick a gun to the back of a white guy at the Malco Quartet cinemas. His gentle soul was impossible for even the hardest criminal to ignore. It was also an unwritten code in Binghampton: Good athletes got a pass. If they didn't want to be part of gangs, then the gang leaders respected that. When bad shit was about to go down in the neighborhood, Desmond would get tipped off: "Dez, you don't need to be around here no more." He'd scatter.

Basketball was his life. He and Penny knew each other from the hallways of Lester and from the courts outside. In Penny, he saw a leader who was going to make it, and a potential outlet for a better life for himself. And so a relationship blossomed. Penny and Desmond played day and night. While Penny had to be home by dark, Desmond had no curfew. He would stay out till 1 A.M. honing his skills.

As a freshman in high school, he played on the varsity team for powerhouse East High. In a game his senior year against Harding Academy, Desmond fought off the flu. He had blurred vision and saw three baskets when he took to the court. His first shot was an air ball. The gym erupted in taunts: "Air ball! Air ball!"

"Shoot for the goal in the middle," Coach Reginald Mosby told him.

From that point on, he caught fire. He hit five straight three-pointers.

In the locker room, Desmond put his head between his knees, covered himself in a towel, and cried. The only thing he wanted was to look in the stands after each made shot to his father—to share that joyous moment between son and father, to know what it felt like to have that bond with a dad. Yet he had never met his father. He was told this one dude in Binghampton was his dad, but he never believed it. Dez didn't look anything like the man, and the guy was an asshole. "Seems to me if he was my dad, he could at least say 'hi.'"

Sobbing after that game, Dez promised himself then that if he ever became a father, he'd never abandon his children.

"He's a man-child. He's tough," Coach Mosby told the local paper after one double-overtime victory in which Desmond scored 23 points.

"I consider myself the soldier," Desmond said simply.

Coach Mosby was the most instrumental man in Desmond's life. He was like that for hundreds of boys over the years. Mosby prowled the East sidelines for more than twenty years, earn-ing the highest winning percentage in city history. "Besides my grandfather, he's the only other male in my life who gave me good guidance, the guidance in life to become a young man. He taught the value of being a man, period. Like the things you should and shouldn't do in life. He instilled the discipline. He made sure you go to school on time. We couldn't wear earrings. You didn't walk around with your shirt out of your pants. He made sure you went to study hall. It was mandatory. You had to be clean-shaven. If you had a curl, you had to get it cut off before you could play for Coach Mosby."

The coach told young Desmond to seek greatness for himself and to prove to his absent father that he was missing something special.

Memphis State coaching staff had invited Desmond to walk on his freshman year, earn a scholarship, and become a starter or valuable contributor off the bench by his sophomore season. The University of Missouri and St. Louis University were on his short list, but the scholarships never came. He was too poor to afford the high cost of a college education if he didn't get a free ride. Without a father to advise him, Desmond didn't know where to turn. He didn't feel like sitting out his freshman season at Memphis: He felt he was too good to do that. After all, he'd netted about 18 points a game for one of the top teams in Memphis. He first went to historically black Lane College in Jackson, Tennessee, where he suited up for the basketball team. But he had higher expectations of himself than Lane. Desmond transferred to Austin Peay State University, a Division I school in middle Tennessee that was known as an upset special during March Madness. Yet the transfer meant he had to sit out for a season, only allowed to practice with the team. He couldn't suit up or travel with the team. It crushed him. He felt he didn't fit in, as a player or student. He longed for home, too. He dropped out of college and returned to Binghampton, the only place he felt comfortable. He continued to take courses at a local college when he could, but when his son, Nick, was born in 1998, he knew he had to find a way to graduate. He went back to Lane to complete what he started years earlier: earn an education degree. Even then, he told friends and family he would one day return to Binghampton to coach at Lester—that his son would help them earn a state championship. "He might be little now," he told friends, "but Nick's gonna be a star." He nicknamed his boy King.

When Desmond took the coaching job as a volunteer in 2008, he walked into the locker room of one of the worst teams in the city, with a 3–23 record. The boys were out of control. They skipped classes. They were failing in school. The previous coach didn't care, nor did the student-athletes—if that term even applied to the boys wearing the black and gold. Desmond recognized that the role of coach extended beyond just X's and O's. In his first year he tried to get the kids to focus not just on the game but on discipline and life around them.

"I told the kids that I earned my bachelor's degree, but I wanted them to earn their master's degree." He wanted them to "do better than me."

The team responded. In just his first season, the team won more than twenty games and earned a trip to the state playoffs, where the Lions lost to a team from rural Lake County called Lara Kendall, one hundred miles north of Memphis, in the far northwestern corner of Tennessee. Desmond had become known around the city for driving his team in his beat-up Saturn sedan, its bumper scraping the ground. The car would pull up outside an opposing gym and his entire team—including several players over six feet tall—would pile out. A family as much as a team.

• • •

Just days before Penny visited him in the hospital, Desmond had drifted in and out of consciousness. He was at stage 4 colon cancer. He'd already had three surgeries to remove part of his intestines and an infection had left him critically ill. He needed emergency surgery to keep the infection from spreading and to save his life.

Fortunately, he couldn't have been in better hands. Methodist University Hospital, in the heart of Memphis, is a state-of-the-art medical center, with 661 beds, where doctors specialize in transplants, brain and spine issues, and cancer. Its most famous patient was Apple cofounder Steve Jobs, who came to the facility in March 2009 for a liver transplant as he struggled with his own cancer battle. The hospital has one of the largest liver transplant centers in the country, and it's consistently ranked as one of the top medical facilities in the South.

For Desmond, the medical campus—a maze of brick buildings with manicured courtyards along Union Avenue—made an oasis for family and friends to visit him. He lacked health insurance, but saving his life trumped the mounting medical bills. Binghampton faced the very real possibility of losing one of the good guys. Family and friends piled into cars for the two-mile drive from Binghampton to visit. They prayed like nobody's business. His son, Nick, and daughter, Ziona, visited nearly every day, but it was hard to even look at him—his body so thin he was nearly unrecognizable to his own kids.

In his room one morning, his fiancée, Inga, sat next to Desmond on the bed. She read aloud the book of Job, the pious man whose faith was put to the test by Satan, the man who refused to curse God even after his ten children were killed and all his possessions destroyed. Job would become infected with painful boils, scraping his flaky skin with broken pottery because he itched so bad. Job's wife begged him to "curse God and die." He refused.

"You speak as one of the foolish speaks," Job said. "Shall we receive good from God and shall not receive evil?"

Yet despite the biblical lesson, Desmond was filled with fear. Inga and his mother, Nadolyn Merriweather Smith—a stout woman with a belief in the Bible that matched her thick frame—told him how much he was loved, how he'd touched them. His mother had come back into his life full-time by the time he was a senior in high school. A medical assistant, she turned her home into a virtual cancer center, taking care of Desmond around the clock. She tried making up for the years she missed in his childhood, dedicating her life to trying to get her son well.

She also scolded him, saying he put basketball before God. He grew defensive. He countered by saying he was doing God's work through basketball, that the boys of Lester would wind up wearing the colors of local gangs instead of the black and gold of the Lester Lions if he didn't try to intervene. His mother could accept that, but she added one last bit of advice: "Share your Sunday with the Lord, not the basketball."

On the day of Desmond's emergency surgery, the waiting room at Methodist hospital was filled with friends and relatives—and fear. People paced. Some went outside to catch a smoke. The doctor eventually emerged from the operating room and asked to speak privately with the family. "I might as well tell you the truth," he said.

Desmond was critically ill and they were forced to leave his intestines exposed to the open air to try to stave off further infection. The doctors hoped to clean the infected area during those two days. It was Desmond's best chance for survival, but the lead doctor explained Desmond likely wouldn't live beyond the next forty-eight hours.

Desmond's mom fell to the floor. "My God!" she screamed. "Desmond's gonna die!"

The news quickly reached the larger community and within a half hour, the waiting room swelled from twenty to more than one hundred. The family had called Rev. Larry Peoples to pray over Desmond. Around Binghampton, he's known as the Prayer Warrior, a man so steadfast that he's got God on speed dial. He, too, was in the waiting room and heard the doctor describe Desmond's open wound. He saw it as a sign: a cleansing of Desmond's soul.

"Rebuke that devil!" the preacher hollered. "He is gonna live!"

Rev. Peoples—whose skinny, 6-foot-2 frame spoke to his own former hoop dreams—looked out over the growing crowd. He saw people he hadn't seen in twenty years, from right after he'd been freed from prison for more than twenty counts of armed robbery. He had changed his ways from notorious gangster to evangelist. Now his veins bled scripture. When he got on a roll, he'd shout, "The Lord's dealing with me!" and everyone knew to step back and start listening.

The Lord was doing something to the reverend right now. His body swayed; his voice bounced off the stale walls and down the long tiled halls of the hospital.

"What y'all crying for?" he screamed. "Not one tear can help Desmond. It's y'all who need to repent so God can hear a righteous cry. God just told me Desmond's gonna be okay. It's you who need to be saved."

In the intensive care unit, Desmond looked near death. An endless line of IVs was hooked up to his body. A ventilator machine wheezed. Most grotesque was his open wound. If you peeked around the curtain, you could literally see his guts.

Outside the hospital, a vigil began. Black radio stations in Memphis asked for prayers. One soldier just back from the war in Afghanistan came to pay his respects. Pimps and drug dealers of Binghampton did, too—like damn, man, how can Binghampton lose Dez. It was one thing to lose guys to drug overdoses and shootings. But why take Dez?

Desmond's mom looked into making funeral arrangements. His team received misinformation. They were told Dez had died. A shock that sent them into a fit of tears.

But amid the wake, a miracle happened. By late Wednesday, with his intestines still exposed, Desmond began to awaken. He scribbled on a pink piece of paper. "Call Inga. Call OneCent," he wrote, referring to his fiancée and Penny Hardaway.

By Thursday—the end of his forty-eight-hour death sentence—doctors had stitched Desmond back up. The procedure was a success.

Desmond still had cancer, though, and would need more treatment in the months ahead, but it was a positive sign he was alive. Friends notified OneCent, as Dez had requested. And that's how the bedside reunion came about.

After four hours of catching up, it was time for Desmond to get rest. He and Penny hugged. "Whatever you need, I'm going to take care of you."

The idea of Penny doing more with the Lester Lions didn't come up. He strictly committed to getting team uniforms. Nothing more.

CHAPTER 4

A Birthday Bash

The smell of ribs, baked beans, Binghampton spaghetti—a concoction of meat, Ragu, and love, the type of soul food that transforms Memphis blues into more like New Orleans swing—swept through the Lester Community Center and across Binghampton. The same facility where Desmond fed the ball to Penny twenty years ago was filled with more than four hundred people to celebrate Desmond's thirty-eighth birthday—and his cancer survival.

The center's indoor gym and classrooms were decorated with yellow and black streamers for Lester's team colors. Signs read: "Happy Birthday, Dez!" and "We love you!" There were so many people gathered that the crowd overflowed from the indoor gym to the courts outside, almost like the old days, when ballers waited for hours to hoop it up.

Desmond was nearly inseparable from his son, Nick. The two shared the same birthday. When Nick was born thirteen years before, the doctor handed him to Dez and said, "That's the best birthday gift you'll ever get."

The two locked arm in arm in the rec center. Nick was a spitting image of his father, but small for his age of thirteen, at just 4-foot-11 and 95 pounds.

It had been nearly a year since the emergency surgery and Nick had seen his dad battle back from cancer. He'd watched his dad continue to endure numerous rounds of chemo. Desmond had slowly recovered and called in his brother, Marty, to help coach the team that winter. Lester won the city championship but lost in the state regionals to Union City.

Many at Desmond's party were checking in with him about the upcoming season. The players who had started with Desmond in sixth grade were now eighth graders, including potential All-American Reggie Green. It wasn't a big leap to think that this year Lester might even win state. They had the talent, and with Desmond's survival, they had the inspiration. And the neighborhood longed for some good news for a change.

Dez with his son, Nick.

The name Lester had become synonymous years before with one of the city's most heinous crimes, in which six people, ranging in age from two to thirty-three, were found dead in a Binghampton home with so much blood splattered that even the most veteran police officers were horrified. Three other children, from four months old to nine, were seriously injured with stab wounds, including one child who had a knife still wedged in his head when police arrived. The killings in March 2008 became known as the Lester Street Murders. So infamous were the killings that the stigma carried over to anything named Lester, including the middle school. The murmurs could be heard in opposing gyms: How close is Lester Middle to the killings? Did any of the kids see it happen? Typical, all they do is kill each other over there. At least that was the prevailing thought in Memphis about Binghampton.

The neighborhood was desperate for something positive.

Over the past year, Penny had continued to rekindle his friendship with Desmond and had stayed in close touch. He had even paid Desmond's medical bills and donated a passenger van, so Desmond would no longer need to overstuff his Saturn sedan with the team.

Penny was also working on a bigger project to help out the community. He was looking to build a $20 million facility in suburban Memphis with basketball courts and classrooms to tutor at-risk kids. His goal was to get the inner-city kids to the suburbs: to teach them to dream bigger dreams. That's what had inspired him as a boy, playing on elite teams that practiced in the suburbs, where he saw manicured lawns and nice homes—a different world from anything he'd ever seen in the inner city, where sirens sounded as much as LL Cool J's "I Can't Live Without My Radio."

His facility was a great plan, but it was not without controversy, as local politicians and civic leaders felt the facility should be built in the inner city and not out in white suburbia. It meant that Penny was forced to spend a great deal of time with lawmakers and other power players to try to secure funding instead of actually coaching kids.

This night, Penny was on hand at Desmond's birthday party to honor his longtime friend and gave an evening-ending speech at the center. He announced he was outfitting the Lester Lions with new, specially made uniforms from his OneCent logo.

"They're gonna look better than the Pittsburgh Steelers in black and gold," he said.

The place erupted with cheers. Penny had promised the uniforms the season before, but Desmond had never gotten around to ordering them because of his cancer recovery. Onstage now, he hugged Penny.

When the crowd faded, Penny and Desmond went to a family restaurant, known by locals as Perkins on Poplar, where they sat at a round table in the corner. Over grilled chicken sandwiches and french fries, they discussed uniform styles, shoe sizes, jersey numbers. They left excited. Lester's boys and girls basketball teams would get warm-ups and uniforms, plus shoes to match, including some of Penny's high-dollar Foamposites. The team would be better dressed than some NBA franchises. They hoped it would provide a spark for kids who had so little. Many of the players were so poor they couldn't afford their own basketball shoes.

A few weeks after their sit-down at the diner, Penny's grandmother died at age ninety-five. He had learned of her death while attending the funeral of the mother of one of his friends. Penny's mom texted him with the news—that Louise Hardaway, the pillar of his life, had passed away quietly.

At his grandmother's service, Penny approached Desmond and

said something about the uniforms—Dez stopped him right there. Today was about honoring his grandmother. Basketball could wait.

Desmond did invite Penny to play at a charity basketball game, called "We Are Family," at Lester Middle School to help raise scholarship money for high school seniors and the Lester Community Center. Desmond hoped it would get Penny's mind off his grieving and it was for a great cause: getting kids to college. Desmond kept Penny hidden from view until the start of the game to shock the crowd.

The gym was filled with more than fifteen hundred people—most dressed in "We Are Family" T-shirts. The sound system blared Sister Sledge. The crowd held hands, swayed, and sang out:

> *We are family*
> *I got all my sisters with me*
> *We are family*
> *Get up ev'rybody and sing*

And, boy, did Binghampton stand up! It was like *Soul Train,* the place was so hopping, everyone dancing and grooving and getting down. The only thing lacking was Don Cornelius and a disco ball.

Bozo Williams, a scraggly man in his sixties with gray hair and a beard, took to the court. He got on his knees, thrust his hips, and gyrated his body with black-and-white pom-poms in his hands. Bozo had studied to become a photographer at Memphis State in the 1960s, before he'd gone the way of drugs. For the last thirty years, his biggest thrill has been to attend basketball games and fire up the crowd. He tossed the pom-poms to the ground and twisted and contorted his body into a letter.

"Give me an *L*!" he shouted.

The crowd roared. And on Bozo went, using his body to spell out L-E-S-T-E-R.

Penny couldn't believe the environment. Lester didn't even have bleachers when he attended in the mid-1980s. Now the school had hardwoods that glistened, bathrooms that worked, and locker rooms with lockers. In an era when schools were cutting back on recess, Lester poured money into the gym to provide an outlet for the kids. The more they played in the gym, the less time they spent on the streets. Gym time was more than jumping jacks and flag football. Here it meant a better chance to survive. One less kid to serve as a cocaine runner at the age of thirteen.

The charity game pitted Lester alum against former players from East High School, the school that Lester was a feeder for and where Desmond attended. In fact, Penny had stunned Binghampton in the 1980s when he chose to attend nearby Treadwell High over East to play with Elliot Perry, the guard known as much for his speed as his goggles and socks up to his knees. He too made it to the NBA.

The announcer talked about the Friday nights of old, between November and March, when there was only one place to be, watching the dominant East High basketball team. "It's time to relive the good ole days!" he screamed.

Players for East rushed the court. The alum representing Lester were announced, except for one. Penny's heart raced.

"Uh-ohhhhhhhh, now!" the crowd chanted.

The announcer told Binghampton to stand up—that they had a special guest in the house, the best player in Memphis history. "PENNNNNNNNNY Hardaway!"

Penny burst through the locker room door and through a line of cheerleaders on the court.

Glancing around, Penny could feel something deeper. He

sensed hope and optimism, Binghampton united like family, just like the motto on this night: We Are Family. The gym was pristine, with "Lester Lions" painted in black and yellow on the wall. Center court was stamped with a lion's paw.

And amid the screams and chants of the crowd, the old playground rivalry was renewed. If there was any team that ever got Penny's juices flowing more than the Chicago Bulls and Los Angeles Lakers, it was the East High Mustangs. Penny rained down so many points during one game against East, as legend has it, the lights literally went out. The gym went completely dark and the game had to be rescheduled.

"Gonna be just like old times," Penny said.

The referee tossed the ball into the air. It was showtime.

Penny didn't disappoint. He may have been a little rusty, but he still had some all-star moves. He shaked and baked. He hit former Lester star Corey Bolton with a behind-the-back pass that made everyone's jaw drop. At night's end, Penny finished with a triple-double.

Afterward, he put his game face away and hung out at the court to catch up with the other players and old friends. He signed autographs for anyone who asked. The night had caught him by surprise. He hadn't had this much fun or camaraderie since leaving the NBA in 2007.

He felt a definite tug—and it wasn't just about the thrill of competition.

Desmond walked with Penny out of the gym and told him that the season had just begun, and that he was struggling more than he thought with the chemo treatments. The team was talented, Dez said, but had lost its second game of the season to Fayette East, a good team in the backwoods about forty miles outside Memphis. Lester lost by a single point.

Dez said he could use some help—that the team needed tips on how to score against zone defense. Penny stopped on the court. He'd been thinking about home for much of the last year. He knew it was time to heed the words of his late grandmother: "Do for your community, do for your people, do what God puts in your heart."

Penny showed up at their next practice.

CHAPTER 5

Penny Meets the Team

The Lester Lions. Left to right, Kobe "the Mayor" Freeman, Demarcus "Black" Martin, Reggie Green (standing in back), Albert Zleh, Xavier Young, Derrick Carnes, Andrew Murphy (partially hidden), Robert Washington, Courtney McLemore, George Bee, Nick Merriweather.

The boys of Lester Middle dripped with sweat. They raced up and down the court, doing layup drills. The orange glow of the fluorescent gym lights flashed off the hardwoods. Coach Dez barked out signals.

"Y'all ain't hustling enough," he said.

At the far end of the court, Penny peeked his head in the door. None of the kids noticed. He and Desmond decided that Penny would show up and surprise the sixth, seventh, and eighth graders. As the players continued to run the court, Penny kept peeping his head in and out of the black metal doors until finally breaking into their practice.

Some of the boys instantly recognized him from the charity game two nights before and sprinted toward him.

But the two best players, Reggie Green and Robert Washington, trailed behind. They weren't sure who the 6-foot-7 guy with the trimmed goatee was.

Reggie was the team's affable star, outgoing, talkative, and smooth. A 6-foot-3 power forward, the fourteen-year-old could outmuscle most teams with his sheer size. He could dominate in the post or use his finesse to pull up on a fifteen-foot jumper. His grandfather was Antoine Richardson, the same one who helped mentor Penny in his youth. Basketball served as Reggie's escape, his refuge away from street life and his mess of a home life. His father had been imprisoned seven hundred miles away in North Carolina six months before. As with many serious offenses, the people of Binghampton have collective amnesia when it comes to specific charges: something about a high-speed chase, his car might've struck an officer, he might've resisted arrest—ya know, ordinary stuff. He also beat Reggie severely before being captured, hurting the boy as much mentally as physically.

His father had been a huge boost for him the previous season, a mainstay at basketball games, and now Reggie's world was shattered. Nicknamed Taz, his father, in his early thirties, turned into the Tasmanian Devil in the stands, so wild and crazy he spun around dancing with joy after each basket his son scored. Taz would race from the stands and sprint alongside Reggie each trip up the court. In his view, Ji—as he called his son—could do no wrong. Taz would shout Ji's name so loud it would bounce off the hardwood floors and through the cavernous gym. "Give it to 'em, Ji!" Taz shouted. And Ji lapped it up. He'd pound his chest after a made basket, point to his heart and back at Taz. It was a way of showing his dad how much he loved him. Taz hadn't been there for most of Reggie's upbringing and had only returned to Binghampton because he was trying to avoid arrest. He lived the life of a gangsta and had never dreamed Ji could get his family out of the ghetto the clean way, by playing ball. But when Dez took his son under his wing, Taz saw big lights and an NBA future for his boy.

But the blue and red lights of the police caught up with him.

Reggie had been living with his aunt before his dad's arrest, but was then forced to move into his grandmother's apartment in a different neighborhood, called Hollywood, a few miles away. The whole situation left him shaken, scared, and confused. Guys hanging out in the stairwells of the building and others on the block jumped on the new kid. Turf wars are real and he was coming from Binghampton, a rival hood. His grandmother, Sheila Harris, fortunately was a tough-as-nails forty-nine-year-old and a worthy combatant, hell-bent on her grandson getting out of the projects. "They were trying to fight him. Everything," his grandmother said. "They were really at Reggie, you know. They started surrounding him at the gym. They were over there double-teaming him because he don't want to be a gangbanger. He's not a follower. He's a leader.

"You got the gangbanging, you've got the ones trying to pull him in and get in his head because he's a young boy. We're surrounded by them. Shit, that's all they do. GDs, Vice Lords, all of them. Grapes, stay right next door. But they don't bother mine because I put it out there.

"The furthest Reggie's ass can go is right here to this curb. I may let him go to the park. But Coach will tell you, when them streetlights come on, his ass got to be right back here: Nine o'clock, he's got to be in the house."

She called the police, she called the gang unit. Whatever it took to keep the pants-on-the-ground, hat-turned-sideways gangbangers away. "I tell them don't mess with my kids!"

His grandmother is known around the neighborhood as the Freeze Cup Lady for hustling Popsicles at fifty cents a pop as a way to keep Reggie and her three other grandchildren under her roof. Reggie's mother is in and out of his life, living just up the street a few apartments away. But as his grandmother put it, the less time she spends with Reggie the better: "Lord, baby, beats his ass. I'm grandmomma hard. But down the road, she's momma hard. She don't play with his ass. He can get away with things with me, but her—oooh, baby—she ain't nice."

Reggie was the team's leader, having played for Coach Dez since sixth grade. But with his father in prison and his downgraded and dangerous home environment, Reggie grew angry and resentful. Who could blame him? He was once an honor roll student, but his grades began slipping in the fall of 2011 as basketball season approached. His blunt-spoken grandma gave him this advice: "Shiiiiit, Reggie. You never know what's gonna happen. Just stay prayed up, ya know. Live from day to day. One day at a time."

Now, in the gym, he looked at his shirt and at Penny. His shirt was from a summer basketball camp sponsored by Memphis Grizzlie star O. J. Mayo and Penny. The images of both basketball players graced it.

"Is that really you?" Reggie asked.

"Yeah, that's me," Penny said with a smile.

"You look different," Reggie replied.

While Reggie was the veteran of the team, this was Robert Washington's first time playing for Lester. He had never played organized ball before this season. He knew the game from playing on the street, at rec centers, and even on an Amateur Athletic Union (AAU) travel team, but that was all about individual play. The concept of winning was wrapped around having the best move to the basket, not about the final score or playing together. At 6-foot-4, Robert Washington had a seven-foot wingspan. His bones ached from growing so fast and at just fourteen it was clear he wasn't done. To older Memphis fans, he resembled a young Keith Lee, the dominant big man who took the Tigers to the Final Four in 1985. To the current generation, he resembled a different hoops star. His long limbs and faded haircut, along with his stellar play, earned him the nickname Little Durant, as in Oklahoma City all-star Kevin Durant.

Robert lived in two neighboring homes a couple of blocks from Lester, one belonging to his aunt, the other his grandmother. Like Reggie's, Robert's dad also sat in prison. His dad had been locked up nearly all of Robert's life, mostly for drug offenses. The homes were a living testament to the saying that it takes a village to raise a child. He was one of twenty kids being reared in the homes. Most days, his uncles sat in lawn chairs under the shade of an oak tree, telling tales and hustling. With so many kids running about and his father absent, similar to Penny's own adolescent experience, there just was no one to push Robert to achieve. His auntie, Charity Washington, nicknamed Shree, did her best but her presence wasn't like that of a male role model.

"The one thing I would hear Robert say a lot is 'All I want is my daddy to be at my games,'" she said. "He's never had that type of figure, never had a normal person in his life, like a dad.

"He's never had anyone motivating him. His father is a street father. His father never took him to the zoo or to the park or celebrated with him at his birthdays. It's all about quality time because boys always want their dads with them. Robert can never say that, because his father was never there."

His aunt pointed up and down the street. "Robert didn't choose the streets. We weren't going to let him do that," she said.

At the Lester gym, Robert stood in front of Penny and looked down at his size-13 shoes instead of Penny's eyes when the two shook hands. Penny noticed Robert's hands were nearly as big as his. "Dude's got some mitts," he said later.

Penny asked who the hype man was on the team.

"Me," said Kobe Freeman.

At 5-foot-6, Kobe served as the team's point guard. Reggie and Robert won the acclaim of superstars by pouring in tons of points. But for every big man, there's a little general who directs the floor, pushes the tempo, and feeds the ball to them.

That was Kobe. He had an ebullient smile and polite manners. Nicknamed the Mayor, he always had something to say, usually positive words to encourage others to do better. He wore jersey No. 1, the same as Penny. A daunting assignment when the NBA star becomes your coach.

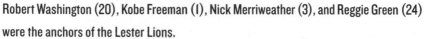

Robert Washington (20), Kobe Freeman (I), Nick Merriweather (3), and Reggie Green (24) were the anchors of the Lester Lions.

Penny could relate to Kobe in more ways than sharing a jersey number. Kobe met his father just three times by the time he was ten. He didn't remember much from those visits, tried not to dwell on the dad he hardly knew. Kobe lived with his five sisters and one brother at a home with his mother in Binghampton. She worked odd jobs that barely paid minimum wage to put food on the table. Kobe had met Coach Dez when he was about eight. "Dez was there before my dad came. I've always claimed him as a father." His dad made an attempt to be more active in his son's life, only after he heard Kobe was a good kid with promising athletic skills. "But it's still the same ole, same ole from when I was younger."

Kobe wasn't shy like Robert and was able to meet Penny's handshake with a big grin.

Desmond's son, Nick, a seventh grader, stood next to Penny. The two looked like the World's Tallest Man standing next to the World's Shortest. Nick's 4-foot-11 build barely came past Penny's waist. Nick possessed a toothy grin and his tuft of hair stood straight up, like an Eraserhead.

Nick had told many of the players about Penny. After his father's recovery, Nick and his dad had stayed at Penny's sprawling house, with its twelve-foot-tall entry way, its waterfalls by the swimming pool, and movie room with leather recliners and a screen the size of a small-town cinema. It was a different world from what Nick was exposed to in Binghampton: lawns littered with trash and gold-teethed, jewelry-flaunting thugs manning corners. Nick lived in a two-bedroom duplex with his father, stepmom Inga, sister, and a stepbrother and cousin, both named J.R. Dez and Inga made it a tidy, peaceful home for what it was. But the neighbors smoked so much dope it came through the vents every time the air turned on; the stove leaked gas daily; the bathroom sink never fully drained. When they brushed their teeth, most of the time they spit in the toilet.

Nick was one of the few players with an active father in his life, yet he had watched as his father nearly died a year before and continued to battle colon cancer with chemo treatment every two weeks. His mother, who lives in Memphis but never had much of a relationship with Desmond, fought off her own battle, suffering from traumatic stomach surgery that nearly killed her.

All of it was enough to crush a child, but Nick witnessed his father's miracle—and gained strength from it. Nick was a soldier, much in the way his father had described himself in high school. The point guard with a lethal three-point shot didn't show any cracks and his teammates rarely knew much about the struggle he and his father faced.

Rounding out the team's eighth graders were guard Courtney McLemore, a science whiz in the classroom and defensive specialist on the court; guard Demarcus "Black" Martin; and utility players Derrick "Ferb" Carnes, Xavier Young, and Albert Zleh. The Zleh family fled war-torn Sudan and wound its way—6,500 miles—to the war-torn streets of Binghampton. There are about nine brothers and sisters living in the Zlehs' nondescript three-bedroom apartment. But the boys are all exceptional athletes, and extremely smart. Albert is fluent in several languages. His older brother rose to become one of the top running backs in Memphis and was being recruited by SEC powerhouse schools to play Division I football.

Aside from Nick, there was one other seventh grader. Andrew Murphy, who struggled with his mother's recent death and fought often with his twenty-two-year-old sister, who was now raising him. His mom was his idol, his rock, his foundation. He lashed out against the world with his mom gone. Hit girls in class, spoke all kinds of nasty to the teachers.

The final roster slots included two sixth graders, Alex Lomax and George Bee. The two cut up in class, but it was easy to get them to listen. It was the older boys who would prove most difficult as the season progressed.

Coach Dez quieted the team so he could formally introduce Penny. He told the team of Penny's NBA career with the Orlando Magic and Phoenix Suns, of the millions he made on the court and from his own Nike shoe line. Dez also told the players that Penny was just like them—that he hailed from Binghampton and had even lived in the Red Oak and Tillman Cove projects. "He's traveled the whole world, so don't never let nobody tell you that you're not good enough. He's living proof that you can achieve greatness in life."

This didn't seem to have much impact on the kids, so Desmond added: "Y'all realize he once scored thirty-eight points on Michael Jordan?"

That got their attention. Penny said he had heard the team was struggling to score against zone defenses. He had instant feedback. When you're a middle school team with two guys who are 6-4 and 6-3, feed it to them.

"I might start coming by more often to see how y'all are doing," Penny said.

Penny glanced at each of the players. In them he saw a reflection of himself from twenty-five years ago: struggling teens in need of positive male role models. He had walked the same streets, lived in the same projects. Every one of them had a story that echoed his.

"I came over and saw the team, and just instantly fell in love with them," Penny recalled. "I wanted to let these kids know that I care. I come from the same situation, and I let them know that they can make it, too. When you have an example who's lived in the same neighborhood, lived in the same apartments, walked the same hallways, that is motivating and it drives them. Their attitudes change. They think, If he can do it, I can do it."

One of Penny's high school coaches, Michael Toney, the one who drove him to the University of Kentucky basketball camp in the summer of 1987, had talked with Penny throughout his NBA career. Coach Toney told him the younger generation could benefit from his guidance—that the Memphis ghetto eats up so many youngsters that it sometimes feels, as mentors, as if they're bailing the ocean, that they need guys of Penny's stature to return home. "He said, 'I haven't been home in fourteen years,'" Coach Toney recalled.

"He could've said 'I'm a multimillionaire'" and never returned, Coach Toney said. "But he came back."

Penny now knew what his old coach meant. He could see how engaged the boys were. They clung to his every word. Robert and Reggie especially caught his eye. He could see they had major basketball talent, but more than anything needed proper guidance in life.

He called for the starting five to take the court. Reggie, Robert, Kobe, Black, and Nick rushed the floor. Coach Dez had said the team needed help scoring against zone defenses. Penny observed them and walked them through a couple of plays.

With a former NBA star in their midst, the team played with an intensity Coach Dez had never seen in them. Reggie rushed to the basket, sailed through the air, and laid the ball high off the glass. He glanced back at Penny and smiled. Black played lockdown defense, as did Mayor Freeman. If Penny was there to help the team score against zone defenses, it was his mere presence that made the team better this day.

Kobe, Black, and Nick—the smallest player on the team— nailed three-pointer after three-pointer.

Before practice ended, Penny asked the team one more question: "Who wants to win the state?"

Every single player, from Nick to Kobe to Reggie and Robert, raised his hand. "That's good to know," Penny said, trying to contain the giddiness he felt inside.

Penny had wild eyes and a huge smile after the players were dismissed for the day. "You didn't tell me how good they were," he said to Dez. "This team is amazing!"

"I didn't want to tell you everything, but they're real good," Dez said. "They're a special group of players."

"I'm gonna be here every day," Penny said, his heart instantly committing him to more than just being a booster. "We're gonna win state with Reggie and Robert. Oh man, what time you want me here tomorrow?"

"School gets out around two fifteen P.M."

Penny showed up early the next day. The first to the gym, with a whistle around his neck. Coach Penny had arrived in Binghampton.

CHAPTER 6

Reshaping Boys

Penny with Desmond Merriweather and Nick.

After a few practices and a 30-point romp over Hamilton Middle, Desmond and Penny decided to trade positions. Penny would take on the role of head coach for the remainder of the season. However, the excitement of having a former NBA all-star as head coach wore off pretty quickly for the boys of Lester. Penny was used to playing and practicing at the highest level and made no adjustments for the middle schoolers. And it wasn't just about discipline on the court. Penny had a zero-tolerance policy. If he or Coach Dez got called to the school, there would be consequences: suspensions from the team and extra drills at practice for everyone. If players pleaded their case or argued for leniency, Penny doubled down. The punishment would get more strict. It didn't matter who it was—one of the stars or a bench player: Rules were rules, meant to be followed, not broken. The players who acted out of line got punished in another way: They sat during practice while everyone else had to run wind sprints and other drills for their behavior. It was meant to drill in discipline, to show that every action has a reaction—that their choices affect more than themselves. It hurts the entire team. In Penny's world, there were no shortcuts.

Coach Dez had tried to instill discipline in the team, but the players often reverted to their bad habits; some would quit when hard times hit. He suspended them for acting up in class and made them sit out for a quarter or two. Penny's new policy was a shock, but initially the kids were willing to listen to a millionaire who'd conquered basketball greatness. Penny was always clear with the kids, though, that basketball wasn't their best bet for getting out of Binghampton. He wasn't trying to shatter dreams; he wanted them to avoid his own academic mistakes. Many of the players neglected their homework. Some slept in class. Others lived from home to home, schoolwork secondary to basic survival. But if any player skipped study hall or their tutorial programs, the entire team had to run sprints for thirty minutes—no questions asked.

"You're a student first, an athlete second," he told them one afternoon. "I want to make sure you understand that education is more than sports. A lot of you put sports before school, and that's not right, man. I can't allow that as a coach. Y'all gotta attend classes and get y'all's grades up."

Yet it was no easy task. You can't reshape the lives of young teenage boys overnight, especially those who have so many forces pulling them in different directions. But you can plant the seeds and keep watering the plants. Drawing on the lessons of his grandmother, Penny brought tough love. He preached discipline and teamwork: Go to school, tutor sessions, and then practice.

"If you're late, you will get disciplined."

Away from the team, he and Coach Dez strategized. They stayed up until the early hours, game-planning and discussing the next day's practice. They set goals for each player to improve their grades. Penny offered a hundred dollars to any team member who made the honor roll. He hosted them at his huge house for team sleepovers. It was all to show them what it means to be a family. At his home, he'd teach them more values: do their own laundry, fold their clothes, make their beds.

"A lot of the kids are just so distracted whether it be at home or whatever. What I tried to do is allow a kid to come over, stay at my home, focus, work on their homework, and let them focus a little bit better—for at least a couple of days, maybe even a week," Penny recalled.

"Robert was getting into a lot of trouble. He was talking a lot in class; he wasn't paying attention. I just tried my best to do what I could do with him: take him away from the situation where he's most comfortable and just give him a little bit more discipline. And the same goes for Reggie." He laughed about how much time they spent at his place: "Robert thinks he has a room at my house."

Penny confided in them about not having a father in his own life—that he used it as motivation to get where he wanted to be in life. "You can make it through anything. Just look at me," Penny said. "You just have to believe in yourself and believe in what you're doing. Don't ever get discouraged about not having both parents there. You still have to live your life and do the best you can for yourself. Use it to drive you. All of the temptations that you're going to come across, deal with it without anger. Use it to motivate you."

He hoped such lessons would set the foundation for all the boys to grow into great young men. He told each one that he wanted them to attend college, with or without basketball.

"There's life beyond basketball," he said, repeating almost the exact line Spike Lee said at the Princeton camp two decades earlier.

A few weeks after Penny had taken over as head coach, Bozo Williams strolled into the gym to address the team. The Binghampton elder well loved for his sideline antics of using his body to spell L-E-S-T-E-R had something on his mind. He was dressed in a gray winter jacket, white sweater, and sweat pants.

"Look at this man, here," Bozo said, pointing to Penny, who stood at his side. Penny wore a black T-shirt that read: FROM THE START. The shirt revealed a tattoo on his right bicep: THE STORM IS OVER.

"This man grew up with nothing. Y'all are growing up with nothing. No clothes on your back. But what you got, Coach, Nike tennis shoes and all that? We didn't have all that when I was growing up. I used to have to buy shoes for three dollars, and these here shoes I got on—Air Force Ones—somebody gave me these."

He lifted his foot to show his sneakers. He let the players absorb his words, a grown man in his sixties unashamed to wear hand-me-down shoes. The boys were dressed in top-flight gear thanks to Penny's connections with Nike.

Bozo Williams practices twisting his body into letters to spell L-E-S-T-E-R.

Bozo spread his arms out like a preacher at the pulpit. His eyes bulged.

"Appreciate what people are doing for y'all, and make something of yourself. Make your mommy and daddy proud of you."

He pointed toward Andrew and got up in his face. "Stop looking so mean all the time." He pointed at Robert as well. "You, too.

"I don't care how much Coach runs you or whatever. That's all a part of being a player—football, baseball, basketball. That's part of it. You've got to get training."

Bozo grabbed Penny by the arm and said Penny used to hate him for rooting for East High School instead of Penny's Treadwell High. "The coach at Treadwell approached me. He said, 'How much they paying you to do all that at East?' I said, 'They ain't paying me nothing. I'm doing this because of the kids.'"

Penny rolled his head back and laughed, as did the players.

Bozo turned serious. He said he and Penny now respected each other, putting aside their allegiances for a bigger cause. "Love comes with understanding," Bozo said.

"Above all else, I'm proud of him, because he's from here." Bozo spread his arms out again. "Hey, wherever you go, you're going to make Memphis and Binghampton proud. Do that!"

Penny picked it up from there. "This community is all we have. This community cares about Lester. We care about the community. If we go around here acting crazy, then we're not only letting ourselves down, we're letting our family down and our community down. We're not going to do that."

Penny was well aware of what the rest of Memphis thought of Binghampton, and he wanted more for the kids.

The tragedy of Lorenzen Wright was probably not too far from his thoughts, either.

Lorenzen Wright's story was similar to Penny's. Local boy who starred at the University of Memphis for two seasons, drafted seventh overall in the NBA in 1996, and played thirteen seasons professionally, including five with the hometown Memphis Grizzlies. Aside from Penny, Lorenzen had the longest NBA career of any other player in Memphis history. His final season came as a bench player with the Cleveland Cavaliers in 2008–2009, playing in just seventeen games on LeBron James's team, which finished with the best record in the Eastern Division. Lorenzen scored 4 points against the Philadelphia 76ers in what would become the final game of his career.

The city, including the kids of Binghampton, looked up to Wright as a hero who had escaped his environment for hoops greatness. He was more than a ballplayer. He was a good guy with a giant heart to match his 6-foot, 11-inch frame. When his eleven-month-old daughter died in 2003 of sudden infant death syndrome, the city grieved with him. It held him in even higher regard when he formed a scholarship fund, in honor of his daughter, for at-risk students who excel in school. Another time, the mother of a nine-year-old Memphis boy died in her home. The boy lived alone in the house for a couple days while his mother was dead. When Lorenzen learned what happened, he stepped in to help the child out financially. Lorenzen feared the boy would end up in the care of the state or in foster care. He made sure that didn't happen.

But on the night of July 19, 2010, at the age of thirty-four and retired from basketball, Lorenzen Wright was marched from a vehicle and into the woods off Callis Cutoff, most likely with a gun to his head. He managed to pull out his cell phone and call 911.

"Germantown 911, where's your emergency?" said senior dispatcher Claudia Kenley-Woods, who had thirteen years' experience at the call center.

She heard a man cuss and then rapid gunshots. Senior dispatcher Chris Rowlson joined to listen in on the emergency call. At least ten gunshots rang out. The dispatchers stayed on the line, listening, trying to glean any more information about what was happening. They weren't sure if what they heard were gunshots or fireworks. They tried to keep the caller on for as long as possible to pinpoint his location. But as they scrambled, the call dropped. Claudia immediately called the number back. No one answered.

The two checked the emergency system's computer mapping display screen to see if the latitude and longitude of the man's whereabouts were traceable. The location couldn't be determined. They had the caller's phone number and the nearest cell tower, but nothing more.

They had no idea the plea for help was from a Memphis icon, no idea the uproar that would come their way.

They decided not to notify police.

In the woods, the 255-pound Lorenzen lay bleeding with two gunshot wounds to his head, two to his chest, and one to his right forearm. He wore a necklace with two tags, and around his wrist he had a designer watch. Spent shell casings of different calibers sat near his body.

Whoever killed him took his cell phone.

It would be ten days later when police found him.

It was the thick of summer when the Memphis heat lingers, so miserably hot the only way to cool yourself is to carry a wet rag and wipe the back of your neck. Anything to try to beat the heat. A cadaver dog combed through the knee-high grass. The discovery was so wretched, so horrible that even the most veteran officers were horror-struck. The stench was suffocating. There in one inch of muddy water rested a man who had once captured the city's heart for his skills on the court.

The tragedy provided instant round-the-clock fodder for a city that loves basketball, and became the focus of talk radio around Memphis.

Amid the city's grief, tensions flared. Many asked the obvious: How could a 911 call in which gunshots were heard go so completely ignored? And the Germantown Police Department dug in its heels, saying the dispatchers had followed procedure. In a city where race always bubbles under the surface, it nearly reached a boiling point. The eastern suburb of Germantown, where the 911 call was placed, is nearly all white, with giant mansions nestled among picturesque southern magnolias and giant oaks. For black Memphis, race was the overriding factor. The 911 dispatchers never notified cops of the emergency call. In the elite white world of Germantown, Lorenzen's plea for help was apparently viewed as just another black man in trouble and roundly ignored.

News reports emerged that pitted Lorenzen's public image against what investigators allegedly were discovering. He was no longer a millionaire. He was a broke man, millions of dollars in debt. His ex-wife, Sherra Wright, told police Lorenzen came to her white-brick home on Whisper Woods Drive in the hours before he was killed, with an unidentified man. She said he left the home with a box of drugs and came back a second time "with a sum of money," according to a police affidavit. At one point, she said she heard Lorenzen say he was going to "flip something for $110,000." She said Lorenzen left her home around 10:30 P.M., just an hour and a half before he was killed. He owned two guns, a shotgun and handgun—and both were missing. Police believe he might've been killed with his own guns.

In another disturbing twist, news reports emerged that Lorenzen acknowledged to the FBI in 2008 that he sold two luxury vehicles, a Mercedes sedan and a Cadillac SUV, to pay off debts. The man who bought the cars had been indicted the year before on drug distribution charges—and was connected to a drug kingpin charged with racketeering and conspiracy in six killings.

Everyone had their own theory as to who was behind the killing and the cops' indifference to Lorenzen's 911 call.

Lost amid the speculation was the most disturbing fact of all: The killer roamed free and police didn't have a single suspect.

The theories, tensions, and conjectures were put aside in early August 2010 when thousands of Memphians—fans and dignitaries, family and former teammates—poured into the Grizzlies' FedEx Forum to honor Lorenzen.

Yet for all the tears and cheerful remembrances, others took to the stage to urge action on the epidemic threatening to tear Memphis apart. Everyone in the arena knew the dark side that Memphis basketball can take. For every player who makes it out of the inner city to the big stage, there are thousands who don't. Many end up in gangs, hooked on drugs, or both. They never make millions like they once hoped. If they ever make headlines once their basketball days end, it's all too often for the wrong reasons—they get killed or sent off to prison.

It wasn't the first time the city had mourned one of its basketball heroes.

Before Lorenzen, there was Baskerville Holmes, once dubbed the greatest name in sports when he played for Memphis State in the early 1980s. He served as the perfect fit to All-Americans Keith Lee and William Bedford on Memphis State's 1985 Final Four team. An affable guy known for his sense of humor, Baskerville was cut in the NBA by the Milwaukee Bucks and played professionally overseas for several years before returning to Memphis in the 1990s to drive big rigs. With his stardom gone, he struggled with drugs and depression. And on March 18, 1997, Baskerville shot and killed his girlfriend during an argument. Then he killed himself. At least two more former Tiger players—A. Maceo Battle and Aaron Price—have died violent deaths.

Other former stars, including William Bedford, who was a member of the Detroit Pistons' championship "Bad Boys" teams, have served hard time in prison for dealing drugs; some are nearly impossible to track down because they roam from home to home, city to city.

Larry Finch, the late former Tiger star who coached Penny in college, once told ESPN that it saddened him to look at old team photos and realize how many former players were dead. "I sometimes look at the programs that we had. I pick up one and look at it and see the guys' faces that are no longer with us—and it kind of hurts." He said the campus, like others across the nation, was hit by an unprecedented drug wave in the 1980s and that many of his players got caught up in those transgressions.

"The drug thing hit the college campuses—like, boom!" Finch said. "All of a sudden, here it is, and we've got a big-time problem. There were a lot of young men, who were disillusioned about playing ball, mixing those drugs together. Guys that are on drugs, they feel they can do anything and not worry about the consequences. Then, when the basketball is over, reality sets in."

Former Tiger guard John Wilfong, a top executive at a financial firm in town, once told *USA Today*, "What people don't realize is it's really hard to get through that glamour at such a young age. You can end up living your life looking back instead of forward."

Lorenzen's death seemed to reflect that: In the end, he was as susceptible as anyone else, a tragic fallen figure who deserved more than the gruesome death that befell him.

Michael Heisley, then the owner of the Grizzlies, told the mourners he was filled with a mix of sadness and outrage "that someone who meant so much to this community and was such a wonderful guy ends up this way."

"We've become more of an angry people," Heisley said, "and it's spilling over with our children, and each generation seems to be getting more violent than the one before it. I hope something like this can serve to take this tremendous group of people that was here and maybe resolve that they'll do something to at least turn the tide a little bit."

Among those who wept that day was Penny Hardaway. He listened intently during the service, reflected on all the friends' funerals he'd attended over the years. He told one reporter he couldn't shake the thought of what happened to Lorenzen: "Every other minute I'm thinking about it because of the way he got killed and the fashion he got killed."

A year later there were still no suspects in the case, but at least there was a coach in Binghampton who was going to try his damnedest to see that the kids there weren't going to end up as victims, too.

CHAPTER 7

The Choice

Coach Dez had seen Reggie Green leaving Lester Middle School a couple of days after basketball tryouts. Reggie was lanky, at just over 6-feet with a faded haircut. Dez wondered why a kid of his size didn't come out for the basketball team.

"Come here, son," Coach Dez said. "What's your name?"

"My name is Reggie Green."

"What grade are you in?"

"I'm in the sixth grade."

Dez nearly jumped out of his skin with excitement.

Dez eyed him over, a basketball coach sizing up his talent. The boy had hands big enough to palm a basketball. Dez knew he was looking at a star. His gut told him not to let Reggie Green escape. This is going to be the best basketball player I ever coach, Dez thought.

He asked Reggie why a boy of his size didn't try out for the team. Reggie told him that the neighborhood kids said he was "too sorry" to play ball, that he couldn't hang on the courts with the good players, that he didn't have a shot. Dez didn't budge. He told him that was a load of crap. He told Reggie to show up for practice the next day. He also made a pledge to his new recruit. "I'm gonna have you be one of the best kids on the team."

A smile the size of the Memphis "M" bridge grew across Reggie's face. He showed up for practice the next day and a budding friendship emerged between player and coach. But the kid needed help. He couldn't dribble. He didn't know the rules of the game. He'd grab the ball and just run up the court. Coach Dez made it priority one to teach Reggie the fundamentals. As a sixth grader, he didn't play much. He'd sit on the bench and observe the game, but he developed a solid shot and nice post moves in practice. And in seventh grade, he emerged as a star. He poured in about 15 points a game and snatched rebound after rebound. His biggest problem was being lazy. He'd take plays off. Sometimes he let his ego get in the way. He'd bark at teammates that he was the star and they should feed him the ball more. Coach Dez told him to calm down and hustle at all times, rather than picking plays here and there to play hard.

Dez told him that's not the way the game of basketball works, that you have to give it your all every trip up and down the court. Dez thought Reggie resembled a young Shawn Kemp, the explosive NBA all-star who wowed fans with his powerful dunks with the Seattle SuperSonics.

Even after all his growth during his seventh-grade year, Desmond wasn't sure how strong Reggie would be in his final year on the team, after having to move to a rival neighborhood and what he'd been through with his dad.

"That dude, he's kinda rough," Reggie's grandfather Antoine Richardson recalled about Reggie's father. "He'd jump on you in a minute. He don't care if you're a man, woman, dog, or a cat. He was just rough like that. They call him Little Taz, as in Tasmanian Devil."

And the devil poured out of Taz one night while Reggie was still in seventh grade. He was worked into a frenzy. Reggie was walking up the hill along Princeton Street when he saw his father seething up the road. His father was cussing and hissing. He held an extension cord. "I got something special for you tonight!" Taz screamed.

His dad had told him to walk his sister home from school, but Reggie couldn't. The young teen pleaded his case. He tried to explain that Coach Dez said he'd have to run steps and do extra laps if he missed any more practices. Taz didn't want to hear it. Reggie had grown accustomed to his dad getting angry. His dad would stay out late and come in with red, lazy eyes. When he drank, he talked all sorts of noise. But this was altogether different.

"Goddamn, boy! I said get in the house."

At 6-foot-3, Reggie towered over his 5-foot-7 dad. But what Taz lacked in height he made up in man strength. He swung so fast and so hard, Reggie didn't see the slap coming. His head rocked sideways and his knees buckled. The pain shot from his head to his toes. Reggie ran into the home of his aunt. The house was too tiny to hide. His dad followed on his heels, shouting again that he had something special in store for Reggie. His aunt hobbled on crutches. She tried to stop what she knew was coming. Taz yanked her crutches. She fell to the floor crying.

What happened in that home next was something not uncommon for the Hood, but no less tragic. A young hothead dad losing his cool and taking it out on an innocent child. Both of Reggie's eyes were black, his nose swollen. Bruises covered his body and choke marks were visible around his neck. In Hood terms, he'd been given Pumpkinhead.

An awful, awful scene. The type of beating no one should have to endure, especially a loving son.

Taz was already on the run from police in North Carolina. He'd been hiding in Binghampton, and now he was on the lam in the community that had protected him.

Word spread across Binghampton.

Reggie made his way to his grandmother's place. Sheila Harris studied her grandson's wounds. "What happened?" she asked.

"Daddy whupped me," he said.

Sheila stopped in her tracks as Reggie recounted the incident. A rage worked through Miss Sheila's bones like nobody's business. She shook her head, grabbed her phone, and called Taz.

"You ain't have no goddamn business hitting my grandson like you hit him. It's okay to whup his ass, but not like that right there," she said she told Taz. "If you ever fuck with him like that again, I'm gonna put your ass clean in jail.

"There's a certain way to whup a child, but don't hit my grandson like that. Ever." Her hands still trembled from being so worked up as she nursed the boy's wounds.

When Reggie's grandfather Antoine Richardson heard what happened, he paced around his house. He and Sheila were divorced and lived separately. Antoine tried to temper his anger. Didn't Taz know what they were trying to do with Reggie?! Antoine had helped Penny with his shot in the 1980s and provided guidance to him through his formative years. Reggie wasn't as good as Penny yet. But, man, the kid had potential. Antoine helped mentor countless boys over the years. He'd try to put boys on the right path. Some chose the road less traveled. Many fell to the ways of the street.

This was different. This was his grandson, beaten by his own daddy. Antoine put word out: Taz needed to pay him a visit.

It didn't take long. Taz showed up stinking of sweat, like he'd wrestled in a pigpen. Antoine sat Taz down, told him to shut his ass up—to sit there and listen up like a man. Antoine wanted to punch him in the mouth, wanted to rip out Taz's heart, wanted to bash his skull into the wall. Antoine had seen his grandson's face, looked at the pain Reggie was in. The boy's eyes were swollen, his mouth cut up, his body bruised. More than that was the hurt of Reggie's soul—a boy shell-shocked by his father's actions.

"How dare a family member turn on one of his own," Antoine recalled telling Taz. "Do not whup this boy like that again. Reggie don't deserve that. That ain't the way you raise kids. All that boy has ever wanted to do was please you—his dad—and you go and beat him like this. If you ever whup him like that again, you will hear from me. And next time, I won't be using my mouth to do the talking."

When Antoine finished, Taz apologized, said he knew he'd done wrong, that he loved Reggie. He had even called Coach Dez earlier in the day and said the same thing. Inside the locker room at Lester, Coach Dez spoke with Reggie. The boy squinted through his black eyes.

"When I saw him, his eyes were swollen, a cut on his mouth," Dez said. "He told me what happened. Just like he said, I was another father figure. He always depended on me. I sat him down. Talked to him. Told him to stay focused. Told him things like this can happen when people are stressed out. Know that your dad will get better with time. He was taking in what I was telling him. He knew I was in his best interest. He wasn't crying. He was still in a state of shock."

Reggie thanked Dez for being there. He didn't know what to think. Confusion reigned. Dez was in the thick of his own cancer battle, but he couldn't help but think about how young Reggie was and the turmoil he faced.

"To get out of Binghampton, you just need to stay focused," Dez recalled telling Reggie. "Do that and you will win in the end."

Word had leaked out to the cops that Taz was in Binghampton. Police patrolled the streets in full force. Taz knew his time on the run was up. He wanted to make amends with his son, before he went away. Arrangements were made for that to happen. He wept and told Reggie how sorry he was, that he wished he could take it all back—that he'd lost his mind in a fit of rage. He said he was going to go away for a long time and wasn't sure when he might see Reggie again.

It would take another couple days before police captured him.

He was hauled to the Shelby County Jail, a drab building that's as miserable as its stale architecture on Poplar Avenue. It's often a holding cell for the city's most violent offenders, a place to make them sit and rot before they're shipped off to serve hard time at maximum-security facilities. Taz had nothing but time to reflect on the mistakes he made. How he messed everything up.

Reggie visited his father a few times over the next two weeks, speaking to him through a video screen on the wall. He was more concerned about losing his father after just having him back in his life than being angry at him. Taz told Reggie to take care of his sister and that Dez was his family now. He told him to keep his head up and don't drop the rock.

Reggie soon moved in with his grandmother in the rival Hollywood community where thugs a few years older than he pounced on him whenever he stepped outside.

What was happening in his life was too much for a boy: His dad was gone, he was living in a different neighborhood, gangsters threatened to kill him. Life is about choices. But even the best kids, placed in a hostile environment, make the wrong decisions.

Dez put Reggie and some of the other Lester players on an AAU team to keep them active as the summer months neared. On Reggie's AAU travel team, half the team was made up of players from well-to-do families. While Reggie was over at one player's house, he pocketed an iPod. The iPod had been left on a table and was easy pickings. The family lived in the manicured white area of East Memphis and often allowed Reggie into their home. Memphis was like that: a city of contradictions. Racial tensions serve as an undercurrent through most everything in the city by the bluff. Yet less publicized but still prevalent is the graciousness of middle-class and affluent families who open their doors to struggling inner-city youth. The city's largest Methodist church, which I once attended, Christ Methodist, with a congregation of four thousand, has pulled together volunteers since the 1980s and renovated hundreds of homes in Binghampton. The most famous example of a family reaching across racial lines was immortalized in *The Blind Side*, when a white family took in a homeless Michael Oher, provided him a home, and guided him along the way en route to NFL stardom. Dozens of families in the city do the exact same thing without fanfare. They take in inner-city kids, offer them refuge, and provide a safe place to sleep, away from gunshots, threats, and intimidation.

At Lester Middle School, Reggie showed off the iPod to friends, including his teammates. Kobe Freeman and Robert Washington played with him on the AAU team. Kobe didn't like what he was seeing. The stolen iPod represented a betrayal of trust that their AAU coach placed in them—for opportunities they could never otherwise experience. He told Reggie what he had done was wrong.

Kobe called the AAU coach, Steve Chandler. In neighborhood terms, he snitched, but his mom and Coach Dez always talked of doing the right thing. He knew he had to let Coach Chandler in on what happened.

Every AAU team in Memphis wanted Reggie to play for them, but the other coaches were motivated for different reasons: They saw cash coming their way from college recruiters if they snagged Reggie early enough. They'd stop at his house, give him uniforms, spare money—anything to try to win him over to their team.

Coach Chandler had known Reggie for more than a year. He'd let Reggie stay at his house on the weekends. The kid had never taken anything from him. "I can't tell you how many times Reggie would call me day and night: He just wanted to come to my house. He's got a place to sleep, he can eat whatever he wants, he can just be a kid," Coach Chandler said. The coach had even befriended Reggie's father, before he was sent to prison. Coach Chandler had watched as Reggie grew mentally under Dez's leadership. Yet here Reggie—a kid with so much potential, so much heart, so much good—was sliding down that path that so many Binghampton teens choose. Stealing a teammate's iPod was unacceptable.

"I cut Reggie loose at first," Coach Chandler said.

It was a tough-love approach. He just wasn't sure if it would work.

In Binghampton, guilt consumed Reggie. After several days, he told Kobe to relay to Coach Chandler that he wanted to play again. Reggie called him up one night. He initially denied stealing the iPod. Coach Chandler cut through the small talk. "I said, 'I heard you want to come back. Here's the deal. You're welcome to come back but you have to make amends.'"

Reggie apologized not just to his teammate, but to the player's mother, too. "When I cut him loose and he came back, our relationship changed. He decided then he was a leader," Coach Chandler said. "He's just a changed kid. When I first met him, he thought he'd go straight to the NBA, pick his favorite gang to be in—that was his rational thinking of how it was going to work.

"For a white guy like me, an outsider, all I can do is have a conversation with him. I can talk with him about not being a perfect kid . . . But coming from me, it's not as important as coming from Desmond. Not that they don't care about me, but it just means so much more from Desmond."

When Dez was hospitalized, Coach Chandler said he got misinformation. He was told Dez had died. His immediate thought: "It is an awful day in Binghampton if that's true. All those kids are going to be lost. He's a gift to those kids."

As for Reggie, he said, "He's a fighter. His future is going to depend on how much he works."

Coach Penny provides tips to Reggie Green. Under Penny's leadership, not only did Reggie's game improve but his grades did, too. Reggie ended the year with a 3.7 GPA and made the honor roll.

It was against this backdrop that Penny entered Lester Middle. He never spoke with Reggie about what his father did to him, but it was not uncommon to hear of such abuse. "I'm sure it was horrifying," Penny said. "Being a kid and your dad is beating you to the point where you're almost unconscious, and you don't know if you're about to die. I can only imagine . . ."

Penny's arrival brought an impact that surpassed Coach Dez's highest expectations. Penny wasn't just pitching in here and there. He gave the kids his personal cell phone number. He provided it to their moms, dads, aunts, and grandmas as well. "When he told me he was all in, that was it from that day forward," Dez said.

Reggie's grandma saw her grandson suddenly dream bigger. Reggie's mother, the one who was all sorts of hard on him, once joked with her boy to call up Penny and ask for fifty bucks. "Aww, Momma, shoot. When I go pro and get rich, I'll give you that fifty dollars myself," he said. His grandma smiled as she spoke.

"I like that about Reggie because maybe if he says he's gonna go pro, maybe he'll work harder at his game. That's my thought: You always gotta work harder because there's always somebody better than you," she said. "That's what I always tell him. He gets so mad when I tell him that."

There were little things beyond basketball. Reggie needed poster board to finish a class assignment. His grandma, the Freeze Cup Lady, phoned Penny, told him she was too broke to buy the material. Penny sent Coach Dez to the store. Reggie completed his assignment. "I have to give a lot of thanks to Coach Dez and Penny," she said.

Miss Sheila never stopped praying for help for her grandson, but she also knew how to work the phones. "I can call Coach Dez and I can call Penny and say, 'He over here acting a fool. He don't want to get his ass to practice.'" Dez would swing by and pick him up.

Life-altering distractions come in many forms. The gangs were one thing; girls were another. It didn't matter that Reggie was just fourteen. He was tall, handsome, and a potential way out. In the words of his blunt-speaking grandma, "He got a little cum drunk, as far as them girls.

"He got a little girl he was liking on, was trying to lie about practice—didn't hardly want to go. But once he did, he'd come home. He'd be happy. That's my guy. We have a great relationship. Once he'd come home from practice, I'd say, 'How was it?' Reggie would say, 'It was aiight, Grandma. I'm glad I went.' I'd say, 'You see what I'm talking about. It ain't worth sitting around here.'"

Dez and Penny weren't dummies. They sat him down for the Talk: the birds-and-the-bees conversation that every dad dreads. It wasn't just a onetime thing. It was constant.

"We had to make sure we kept our eye on Reggie, like 'We're not going to let you take the wrong path in life as far as dealing with girls,'" Dez said. "What we would tell him and the rest of the team is look at your community, look at Binghampton. Y'all know a couple of these young ladies who got babies by some of these guys who play ball. Look at the young ladies and look at the guys now, and look at the position they're in. They didn't fulfill their dreams as far as going to college. Don't take the path that they took. This place is like a pit. You either get sucked in or you make it out. You choose.

"We had to talk with Reggie a whole lot as he was getting better and better. Because the girls were after him. They think: If I deal with him, that's our ticket out of here. And we tell him and the rest of the team: You're not the ticket for the girls. You have an opportunity to put your family in a better situation. That's the goal."

Temptations lurk around every corner, Penny said, for a rising basketball star, especially in the neighborhood. "It's overwhelming because you're so young and everybody's coming at you so fast. Everybody wants to be your friend," he said. "If you don't have a stable household, you can fall victim to a lot of the women, the drug dealing. You can get in gangs. A lot of what was going on back then when I was growing up was stealing cars. It was just a reckless neighborhood, because you have nothing and you've got to go out and take something. It's an unbelievable situation. It really is.

"I relate to the kids because of my upbringing. I grew up without a mom and dad being there, and that's how I understood what was going on with these kids. It made it easier for me to communicate with them."

The other star of Lester, 6-foot-4 center Robert Washington, was having to split time between two neighboring homes. His grandmother's house was simple but well kept with white asbestos shingles, a single chimney stack poking out from the middle of the roof. Gravel was strewn from the street right up to the back door, a giant oak tree providing ample shade against the smothering southern heat. Most afternoons, his twenty siblings and cousins—ranging from toddlers to teens—moved in ad hoc style between the grandmomma's house and the neighboring home of Auntie Charity Washington, whom everybody called Shree. It wasn't an ideal situation for a teenager who just wanted a definite space to call his own, but it was better than being homeless.

Shree loved her nephew, a beautiful boy with a long, angular face and broad smile that gave him looks like his aunt. She was raising four children of her own, but always made time for Robert. She would walk him the two blocks to school, along with the slew of other children. She liked Robert long before he became a basketball star, because he was a quiet child, sweet and well-mannered. He was also a practical jokester who earned the nickname Goofball for his silliness. On a street where gang members strolled up

and down at all hours looking to make a deal, she was glad Robert
had so far managed to stay clear.

Nicknamed "Goofball," Robert Washington led the team in scoring, averaging 23 points
a game.

"He don't give me no problem at all," she said with a smile,
revealing her four gold teeth. "He don't curse. He don't run the
streets."

Yet she worried about him as he entered his early teens. In
school, he was just getting by with C's and D's. "He was struggling
at school and Penny checked in on him at his classes. His struggles
were more in his life lessons." His father had been in and out of
prison so much, Auntie doesn't even remember what his father
is currently incarcerated for. But Robert longed for his father's
love—for his dad to take him to the zoo, to celebrate his birthday,
to do the types of things a father is supposed to do with his boy.

"You have to understand young fathers need to talk to their
boys out here," Auntie recalled. "Regardless if they're twelve, fif-

teen, or eighteen, they still want their fathers in their lives. You never get too old to want your father or mother. So they're always going to grow up not knowing: Why isn't my father in my life? Why didn't my father ever come to my games? Why didn't my father ever do this or that?"

Robert's aunt, uncles, and grandmother rooted for him at games. His mother, who was in and out of his life, attended games, too. But the one person he so longed to see in the stands was behind bars. "That's the only thing he would say he really wanted, for his dad to be there. He'd say that all the time," Shree said.

And that's why Penny's arrival was so vital. He became more than a coach. He became the surrogate dad Robert never had. He took the boys shopping for clothes, to dinner, to the movies, to NBA games to see the Memphis Grizzlies. At Broadway Pizza in Binghampton, he lectured them about grades. "Your grades better be good," he told the team. He talked with them about not being so angry about not having fathers in their lives. Penny told them his story—that he met his dad only a few times in his life when he was a boy.

"Use it to drive you," he told the team. "Use it to motivate you."

Auntie marveled at the transformation she witnessed Robert going through: a struggling teen into a budding young man. "You could tell he needed a certain type of father's love in his life and Penny came right on in and changed everything.

"To me, that's a lot. I'm struggling and you come help me out. Whether you got a whole lotta money or not, still you're helping my child and ain't nobody else helping him out. That's a big thing to me. He did things a father should do for his own child."

But nothing came easy. Robert wasn't used to being disciplined, to having somebody tell him what to do. And Penny was always getting on him, for talking too much in class, for not hustling enough on defense, for being lazy. Penny would tell him to use his seven-foot wingspan to grab rebounds and block shots—to be a beast on the inside. But every time Penny raised his expectations, Robert rejected them.

He quit eight times.

Every practice began with rigid running drills—suicides, wind sprints, and others. Robert would complain that his head hurt, that his ankle was sore, that his stomach was upset—anything to avoid running. When Penny wouldn't buy his excuses, Robert would storm out of the gym, slink down Jackson Avenue, and sneak into the home of his aunt or grandmother. He would hole up in a room without saying a word.

Most of the time, Auntie didn't know Robert had quit, until a parade of teammates would show up at the home. "You know Robert quit today?"

"What? He quit again?"

Auntie would search both homes and find Robert hiding in a room, typically his grandmother's.

She would then march his ass back to school to apologize.

"He didn't mean no harm," Auntie would say. "He's just lazy. That's all."

But there would be a ninth time that Robert would quit and even Penny wasn't sure if he would return.

CHAPTER 8

The Big Test

Penny carried through on his pledge to get the Lester Lions new uniforms. These weren't just any jerseys. They were works of art, the Armani of basketball uniforms: dry fit, hand-stitched embroidery bearing Penny's OneCent logo. Just slipping on a jersey made the players feel like they were driving a Bentley. Paired with shorts that drooped below the knee and warm-ups with a Lion emblem across the chest, shit was fly. They also had fifty-dollar compression sleeves for their arms and thighs, making them look more like pros than kids from broken homes. And before almost every game, Penny handed out Nike basketball shoes straight out of the boxes. He purchased the kicks with his own money from the Nike factory in Memphis. The kids were sporting Chris Bosh, LeBron James, and Kobe Bryant shoes. But everyone's favorite were the specially designed Foamposites, Penny's shoe. The Foams had a yellow sheen with black highlights and fit snug like a BMW on their feet. Reggie Green dunked harder. Nick Merriweather ran faster. Kobe the Mayor jumped higher on his shots. The Hood kids were suited up in more than a thousand dollars' worth of gear. Hell, Penny's Foams could fetch upwards of a grand alone.

It might seem dangerous, even naïve, to outfit boys of little means with top-flight gear. When Penny's shoes hit shelves in Orlando in 2012, riots broke out. His shoes are still in that much demand, ones where guys get whomped for what's on their feet. But in Binghampton, it was known by everyone: Nobody was to mess with the boys of Lester—or their shoes. Plus, it would be pretty stupid to walk around in the Lester Foams, since only about twenty people had them. Big Slaw Dog might track you down and pound you with his fists, which were tougher than iron.

Big Slaw Dog protecting the neighborhood.

At his first game with Lester, Penny purposefully sat behind the bench in the stands, acting as an assistant to Coach Desmond. The team responded instantly to having him there and blew out local rival Hamilton, an inner-city school in South Memphis, by more than 30 points. He offered pointers throughout the game, whispering to Desmond every now and then. He didn't need to get too involved because the team played so aggressively. A couple of days later, Dez told him it was ridiculous to have an NBA all-star sitting in the stands. He officially, but without ceremony, handed over the head coaching duties to Penny. "He's the better coach. I don't mind being Lil Penny," Dez recalled.

"I was all in from that day forward," Penny said. "I wanted to help him first of all, and help the kids, my school, my neighborhood."

Penny would now be the head coach, but they would be sharing the responsibility of leading the kids to a state championship. Their immediate goal was to keep opponents under 10 points, a seemingly absurd task. But the Lions did just that almost every game, against Georgian Hill, Treadwell, and Cummings—all nearby inner-city schools. They smashed the Memphis Academy of Science and Engineering, 64–7, nearly shutting them out in the first half.

Desmond had been coaching a talented team and he had put together a strong program, but Penny brought real vibrancy and an urgency to win. He was a younger version of his grandmother, using her tough-love approach to coaching. He enforced academics as much as athletics. He made sure those who needed tutors attended their training sessions. "You got sick with cancer and you got soft," Penny jokingly told Dez one day after practice.

"He's a stickler," Dez recalled. "He's Binghampton to the core. That's why I need him beside me, because I knew the things I wanted to do but the kids wouldn't always listen. Penny's got the energy and willpower to carry through with punishment. At rough times in practice, he'd say, 'You know I'm gonna get on them right now.' And he'd lay it on them like his grandma."

Heading into the Christmas break, Lester had improved to 9-1, having recovered from the early-season loss at Fayette East. The holidays are a difficult time and many families struggle to buy presents for their children. Penny helped out by hosting a holiday dinner at the Lester Community Center, dishing out food to hundreds of families. He also gave presents to each team member: their very own iPods.

The MAM Christmas Classic brought together dozens of schools, both large and small, to play for city bragging rights.

Were the Lions as good as Penny and Dez believed?

In their opening game, Lester cruised against an undermatched school named Appling, a mostly white school in the suburb of Bartlett. But it was the next team that Penny was most interested to see how his team would react. Ridgeway played in the state's upper division for big schools and was ranked as the top middle school in Memphis. The team was led by a pair of dynamic guards. Kevin "Lucky" Cheatham was considered the city's best middle school guard. He could do it all: pass, dribble, shoot, and play lockdown defense. He had a good head on his shoulders, a well-disciplined player who followed through on his coach's orders. Playing alongside him was another top guard named Romero Hill, nicknamed Red for his tuft of red hair. He punished smaller guards with quick bursts of speed to the basket and a nasty crossover dribble that allowed him to free up space for his three-point jumpshot. Penny worried that the size of those two would cause problems for his much smaller guards.

When the moment arrived, Lester pounced. The little guys from Lester wanted to stake their claim to being the best in the city, no matter if Ridgeway was the bigger school. They wanted to send a message early and often: that Binghampton basketball was back, better than ever.

It started with the opening tip-off. Lester sensed an overconfident team, and they were poised to push Ridgeway to the max. Seconds after the game began, Reggie Green caught the ball at the free throw line and immediately found Kobe Freeman for an open three-pointer in the corner. The next trip up court, Reggie hit Robert Washington down low for a turnaround bank shot for a 5–0 lead. Ridgeway lost the ball out of bounds on its next possession. Kobe raced up court after the inbounds pass and scooped the ball in for an off-balance layup. Lester immediately got the ball back and went down to Reggie on the block. He gave a shot fake, caught the defender in the air, and passed to Robert for another layup. Moments later, Reggie countered with an easy bucket.

Just like that it was 11–0. Ridgeway countered with a few buckets, but Robert soon reeled off 8 more points in a span of about a minute.

The best big school in Memphis was getting dismantled. Ridgeway's powerful guards tried to lead a charge. They got several steals and quick baskets, inspiring a brief but uneventful comeback. The early lead was too much. Robert manhandled Ridgeway's post players, even draining a three-pointer in the second half. On another possession, Reggie streaked through the lane, flew through the air, and tried to dunk, but the ball rimmed out. Robert muscled for position, tipping the ball about five times to keep it alive, before grabbing the rebound and putting it back in.

Everything clicked.

The team not only stood the test but they humbled Ridgeway.

The final: Lester 59, Ridgeway 44. Their record improved to 11-1. The Lions held a ten-game winning streaking, eight of them with Penny. In the locker room Robert and Reggie danced around giving everyone high-fives.

Penny was all smiles, too, and told the players he was glad to see them this focused.

But the highest of highs can be followed by the lowest of lows. The Lester Lions were about to be humbled themselves.

Lester's following tournament games were against two other big schools, Lowrance and American Way, which always seem to rank among the top basketball programs in the city. Both teams had scouted Lester in its win over Ridgeway. Their assessment: The key to stopping Lester was to shut down Robert. They both double- and triple-teamed him, packing in a zone defense to force Lester's guards to make three-pointers. The games mirrored each other. Lester held its own in the first halves, but Lowrance and American Way used their size, strength, and conditioning to wear down Lester in the second halves. Lowrance won by about 15.

And when Lester got behind by 10 points against American Way, the Lions quit. American Way was powered by Dedric Lawson, a 6-8 giant who could dribble, shoot from the outside, and dominate inside. Dedric was already getting looks from Division I schools. It was as if Reggie and Robert were intimidated. Both walked up on defense, letting American Way score uncontested layups. The two stars barked at their guards for not getting them the ball. When the two subbed out, they bickered on the sidelines, saying they needed to be back in the game, not on the sidelines. They let their egos get in the way of the team.

The tension spilled over. Kobe, Black, and Nick kept turning the ball over, and they missed open shots. Penny encouraged the players from the bench, but he felt helpless. He wanted to throw a uniform on, get the ball, and take over the game as he'd done so many times during his playing days. This was a new feeling, an uncomfortable one that every coach endures when they first get on the job. All Penny could do was give advice and hope for the best.

It wasn't a high-scoring game, but American Way also beat them by almost 15 points.

It's easy to cope with wins, when everything is going your way and everything is falling into place. But it's losses that test a team.

And the Lester Lions had just lost two in a row.

They still had a strong record at 11-3, but they were now beatable and vulnerable to other schools trying the same tactic. The team dynamic was clearly in jeopardy. Reggie and Robert had become too selfish. They put themselves ahead of the team, caring more about the amount of points they scored than the final outcome. In the locker room, most of the players looked at Coach Penny. Reggie and Robert listened but glanced at their feet, the walls, the lockers—anywhere but at Coach, afraid he'd single them out. Deep down, they knew they deserved whatever tongue-lashing Penny might deliver.

Penny spared no one. He hammered the whole team for quitting. He told them that no matter how much time is on the clock, you don't give up. You play through pain. He emphasized that you never know when the team is going to make a run and come back to win.

So don't quit, he told them.

Penny blamed himself for not anticipating the zone defense. That's why he had first visited the team. Dez had specifically sought his help with teaching the players how to score against zones, and in his first big test Penny failed. He gave himself the task of spending the remainder of the holiday analyzing each player and figuring out how to overcome the big guys being double-teamed. The players needed to be much more disciplined in their decisions.

A reenergized Penny burst into the Lester locker room after the holiday break. He had brooded over the two losses in recent days and worked on figuring out how to retool the team. It was time to put the games behind them and work doubly hard in practice. He said he was adding extra running drills to get everyone conditioned at the highest of levels. The Lester players were quicker than everybody. If they built up their endurance, nobody could stop them. Penny told the players the holiday tournament "showed us what we were made of."

"The big schools, they play against good competition all the time. We kind of get complacent because we play the smaller schools."

The team had prepared well for Lowrance and American Way, "but we didn't play our game," Penny said. "I felt we had the better team in both games, but we didn't stick to our game plan. We can't have everybody on the team, especially the starting five, be off on one night and then not be playing D.

"What happened in those two games? You were all off. And then we weren't playing any defense. So when you're not playing on both ends of the court against a good team, you're going to lose."

Penny urged the players to refocus and not lose sight of what they hoped to accomplish: win the rest of their games and capture the title. Take every game one at a time, but don't forget about that nugget at the end of the season—how great it would feel to bring the title to Binghampton.

Penny was tired of having players not give it their all during practices. He felt the team was being lazy, that the lessons he and Coach Dez were trying to teach them were not sinking in.

"From this point forward, we're going to have all kinds of craziness going on on the team. But the one thing that we've got to do—the people that's going to be here, the people that's going to be on that floor—we've got to be playing for one another."

He took the chalk and wrote the team's motto on the board.

ONE for all
ALL for one

"This means something."

Penny let the words linger like a fadeaway jump shot. "Obviously it doesn't mean nothing to y'all when you get mad," he continued. "Y'all say this every day. Why? Why do you say this?"

Silence filled the locker room. Nobody wanted to speak.

He called on Demarcus Martin, the player nicknamed Black.

"Why do you say this, Black?"

"Because we mean it," he responded.

Penny disagreed. He said there were certain elements on the team who "don't mean it." He didn't mention Reggie and Robert by name. He didn't need to; everyone understood.

He asked again: "Why are you saying this: One for all, all for one?"

"Family," Kobe said.

"It's supposed to be, but as you can see, something different goes on every day. Right? Am I right or wrong?"

Multiple players responded: "Right."

Penny circled "One for all, All for one" on the board.

"Do you think this right here is involved with what those people are doing?"

Players: "No, sir."

He spoke of staying united, of staying committed, of staying together as a team.

"This means something right here. We ain't saying it just to be saying it. Y'all gotta genuinely care about each other. We keep having to say the same thing over and over again. We've got the best team in our league to win the state, but this right here is going to keep us from winning it."

He drew lines connecting the two phrases.

"If we don't do the right thing, somebody's gonna sneak up and beat us that shouldn't. And we'll be looking back, saying, 'Man, we should've won state.' And it'll be all because of the attitudes we got on the team."

He shook his head. "The different attitudes," he said with an air of disgust. "Everybody's going through something. You know what I mean? That's the only negative I'm going to say about that, because we're moving on."

From now on, he said, he wanted no more infighting—Binghampton and Lester are family, and it should never be forgotten. "When the bench goes in the game, the starters need to be happy for the bench. When the starters are in the game, the bench needs to be happy for the starters," he said.

"We have one goal: Win the city first, then win the state."

Penny laid out the plan against their opponent, Hamilton Middle. Nick needed to be aggressive, to play his game and take his shots when they were open. He said the other guards, Kobe and Black, needed to launch threes when they have them. But if they're guarded, he said, dump it down low to Robert.

"Be smart, play your game," he said.

When he was done with his speech, he shouted, "Bring it in."

The players clapped in unison, hopped up and down, and piled their hands on top of one another. Coach Dez led them in the Lord's Prayer, ending with:

God is king,
Power,
Glory,
Forever.
Amen!

Lester took to the court and pounded Hamilton Middle. This was an unleash-a-can-of-whup-ass, grab-your-family-jewels beat-down. The lead at halftime stood at 26–8, a yawner. It was time to fetch popcorn and a corn dog. Because it was lights out. Nah-nah-nah-nah, *good-bye*!

Lester was pimpin' to another win.

The Lions stretched the lead to 40–17 by the end of the third quarter. Penny and Coach Dez were pleased. They tried to keep from smirking. The Lester crowd was hopping and popping and jaw-jacking. This was what they longed for. The way they knew the Lions could play.

But basketball is a game of runs. Leads can vanish in an instant. A single player can get hot and single-handedly rally his team. And teams leading by a huge margin can become overconfident, allowing opponents to chip away. When the fourth quarter began, Lester's play turned sloppy. It was as if they suddenly forgot how to play, or were too stubborn to carry out Penny and Dez's mission. The guards turned the ball over. Reggie and Robert, as usual, stopped hustling. Hamilton seized the momentum, charging back, riding the play of one of their star guards.

Lester ultimately won the game, 54–42, but Penny was disgusted.

Penny has a gentle way about him, even when he's ripping on the players. He's not a foot-stomping, blood-curdling Bobby Knight type. He speaks in a soft but direct tone. He did just that this day in the locker room.

"When somebody starts pressuring us, we start going crazy," he told the team. "And all of a sudden, Robert and Reggie don't want to rebound and block shots no more at the end of the game.

"I don't get it. I don't understand. Y'all need to have some kind of leadership and some kind of toughness in you." He stretched his arms out, told them to never let up—to go for the jugular when the opportunity arises.

"When you get them down twenty points, get them down by

forty. It's almost like you know you're gonna win the game and so you just go through the motions. And then when it's time to win the game, they put pressure on us and y'all fold."

Penny was dressed head to toe in black—black dress shirt, black tie, black slacks. And he was singing a dire tune to match his black outfit. The chalkboard next to him still displayed defensive tips:

1. Press
   - Know your area
   - Traps have to be great
   - Hands up

2. Man to man
   - Lock up

3. Zone
   - Hands up

"We were up twenty and they walked us all the way down. At the end of the quarter, they felt they could've won the game."

He singled out the main guards: Black, Kobe, Courtney, and Nick. They weren't playing with cohesion. On inbounds plays, they needed to work together—to stack up and then fight to get open like they practiced time and again. Instead they were all over the court, resulting in Reggie lobbing in poor pass after poor pass, which spurred the Hamilton comeback. "I've been telling you this all year," Penny snapped.

He asked for Coach Dez to read out game stats. Dez noted that Hamilton's scrappy guard netted 16 points in the fourth quarter alone. Penny shook his head. "We can't even stop one dude!"

He turned to Reggie and Robert and lectured them for playing soft, not rebounding on defense, not dominating on offense. He said other schools watched them lose two games over the holidays. "They're not scared of you anymore."

He told Robert that the man guarding him was holding his jersey, shoving him out of the paint. Penny wanted to know when Robert was going to man up and stop being such a pushover on defense: "We'd rather play ten feet off people."

"We won, but now is the time for us to make that Run that we've been talking about, and we ain't doing it. If you know anything about those big schools we've played, it's that when it's crunch time, you've gotta play D.

"We ain't stopping nobody no more. We let that team—*Hamilton Middle*—score twenty-five points in the fourth quarter," he said.

Exasperated, he hollered, "That team!"

"We're supposed to beat them by thirty points. . . . If they had just believed in themselves from the very beginning, they probably could've given us a tough game. They didn't believe they could play with us, until you started turning the ball over."

Coach Dez chimed in: "They were scared in the beginning."

"We're gonna see how y'all handle the pressure tomorrow," Penny said. "We're gonna see whether y'all fold." Lester had their main divisional rival, Vance Middle School, slated for the next afternoon.

"Everybody in," Coach Dez said.

"We're trying to make this run to the state. You can't win the state like that," Penny said.

Kobe the Mayor counted out one, two, three. Everyone in unison shouted, "One for all! All for one! All for Lester!"

Reggie admitted to playing "kind of soft" and hoped to recover with a strong game the next day against Vance. A lot of Vance players were in the stands at the holiday tournament when Lester lost and liked what they saw. "They ain't got no respect for us no more," Reggie said.

Before Penny left the locker room, he said he was concerned about his team's heart during clutch time. It seemed like a never-ending story: letting up when the game was on the line.

"Right now, we're just trying to get our focus back and trying to make this run to the state," he said. "We're the best team of the small schools, but we don't have the focus all the time that we need to have to win the whole thing." He pointed to his head. "If we keep that focus, we'll win easily."

The Lions rolled into Vance unsure of what to expect. The players had learned over the holidays they were no longer invincible, and the coaching staff wasn't sure of the toughness—mental or physical—of their team. At the start of the season the *Tri-State Defender* had picked Vance, a school located in the South Memphis Hood that looked more like a prison than an educational institution, as a sleeper team that could win the state. But Lester went into Vance's gym that night and pulled off a tight victory, to improve to 13-3.

The Run had begun.

CHAPTER 9

Academics First

Lester students are greeted by a mural of Martin Luther King Jr. and First Lady Eleanor Roosevelt when they walk through the doors. "The time is right to always do what is right," a quote from King says. "The future belongs to those who believe in the beauty of their dreams," reads the quote from Mrs. Roosevelt.

To the right of the entrance is a sign taped with a crossed-out handgun. Right next to it is a bright mural with happy faces, Memphis buildings, and "LOVE" written on a blossoming flower. The yin and yang of Memphis. The brick school building with wide halls, tall ceilings, and large windows has remained the pride of Binghampton since it first opened its doors in 1956 as a school solely for blacks. The mere mention of the name Lester in Binghampton brings wide smiles.

"There's something about that name Lester and the rich tradition behind it," said Monica Clark-Nunley, a seventh-grade reading teacher. "Grandparents and parents went here. If your parents went to Lester, you want to do the same thing and you want your kids to do the same thing. Some people would ask, 'Why?' But it's that heritage and bond they have within this community. That's why they choose to come back. It was the pride of the black community."

"Who was Mr. Lester?" I asked residents. Most people shrugged, said they didn't know. Some gave blank stares. A few said they believed he was "some white dude." A quick spin to the Memphis library verified that: a photo of a sharp-looking man with receding hair and a quizzical look about him. William Charles Lester was an architect who specialized in designing schools, mansions, and apartments throughout Memphis. Among the schools he conceived was White Station, one of the few public schools in Memphis that has a diverse student body these days. He left his footprint on Glenview Presbyterian Church, Gray Road Baptist Church, and the Baron Hirsch Synagogue, the largest synagogue in North America when it was constructed in the 1950s. Two of the city's nicest apartment complexes built around the 1920s, Overton Park Court and the Gilmore, with garden apartments and panoramic views of the city, were the brainchild of W. C. Lester. Mr. Lester died at the age of eighty in his home in the Gilmore in 1960.

He would be proud to see that the school building that bears his name has stood the test of time, having served generations of children in Binghampton. But more than fifty years after Lester opened, the challenges remain daunting, arguably even more so than in the days of segregation.

Of the seven hundred children enrolled in the pre-K through eighth grade program, nearly every child lives in poverty. Most children's first meal of the day is eaten at school and their last meal of the day is served at the cafeteria. Fathers are scarce. In Binghampton, it's atypical to have both parents in your life. If the kids are not being raised by a mom, then grandmas and aunts rear the children. Sometimes it's a bit of everybody pitching in, including the teaching staff. Parents get jailed, some disappear. The kids bounce from the crack-infested projects to homes crammed with brothers, sisters, and cousins.

"During the season, a lot of the kids are just so distracted, whether it be at home or whatever," Penny said. "I want to do things that are life changing for the community and for the kids in the community.

"I wanted to make sure the kids understood that education is more than sports. A lot of them would put sports before school. And if you allow them to do that, then they will. I would tell the kids—*education*—you have to have that to move forward in life."

That advice had been lacking in his life coming along in Binghampton, especially from men. His grandma preached about getting good grades, and guys like Antoine Richardson and the Duck stressed the importance of doing well in school. But it sure didn't seem that important: Everyone else was saying he was gonna be the next Magic Johnson. He slacked off and nearly flunked out of high school. That lack of discipline could've cost Penny's whole career. Now grown and able to reflect on his own life lessons, Penny saw *not basketball players* but vulnerable teens who needed guidance. And he saw a hardworking teaching staff almost overwhelmed by the scope and magnitude of what they faced.

For Lester teachers, it's difficult to stay in touch with parents or whoever is raising the students. A cell phone number provided at the start of the year changes three, four, five times. You can't send a letter home expecting a signature—because many of the guardians can't read. Drug abuse, teen pregnancy, and domestic violence are rampant in the neighborhood. Kids fall asleep in class, often because it's the only quiet time they get. Gang affiliations often take root in the middle school years.

The disarray of the children's home environment is reflected in test scores. In 2010, just 2 percent of Lester's eighth graders were proficient in math; only 7 percent could read at grade level, according to the Tennessee Department of Education. In third grade, none of the students were proficient in reading. The other grades tested equally poor. Sixth graders scored 4 percent proficiency in math and reading. Seventh graders ranked 4 percent in math and 5 percent in reading.

"I had a child tell me, 'I don't need all this, because my momma gets so much in food stamps a month,'" Clark-Nunley recalled. "I said, 'What if they cut off your food stamps? How are you going to live? How are you going to survive?

"I grew up in a household with two parents, both educators, and I value education. For me to come here and see these children not value what I have, it upsets me. I don't have a wealth of money, but I have a wealth of knowledge that I can give these kids and, if you sit still long enough, I can give you the world."

To try to stop the bleeding, the lower grades were being turned into a charter school for the 2012–2013 school year. The aim is to catch children while they're young, get them interested in learning at an early age, before sending them on to the middle school. But the plan is not without controversy. Veteran teachers who'd put in years at Lester got discarded. Yuppie college kids from Duke and other top universities with no teaching experience and no familiarity with the community were parachuting in—and likely would flee when they saw what they were up against.

Whether the new charter school works is anyone's guess.

It's been like this for thirty years—a revolving door of new programs, new teachers, and new principals trying to better the quality of education. In the 1980s, Lester was one of five schools in the nation participating in a program called Apple Classroom of Tomorrow, when the computer giant paid for a computer lab and offered students home computers to try to improve literacy and make learning fun. The only problem: Most parents didn't know what to do with the computers, nor did some of the older teachers. Long-term gains were not made.

In 2001, with students in every grade struggling to read and write, the Memphis school system brought in a new principal and gave him free rein to do anything he could to improve the learning environment. Muffins for Mom and Donuts for Dad events were tried to lure parents in to get more involved in their children's education. The principal put special emphasis on improving literacy. "Reading is more than fundamental. It's absolutely necessary," said Ed Gardner, the principal at the time. "I want every child to be able to read with comprehension and develop a lifelong love of learning. I firmly believe if I teach these young people to read, the test scores will rise accordingly."

They didn't. Nothing worked. More than a decade later, the school had not seen any academic improvement—at least on standardized tests.

Clark-Nunley said she often wonders "where did education go wrong," but she doesn't have time to dwell on the answer because she's too busy trying to get the children in her classroom interested in schoolwork—a daily struggle.

"You have to be able to know the children," Clark-Nunley said. "My thing is I still have high expectations no matter what's going on in your life. When you come in my classroom, I expect you to do the work."

Most of her seventh graders tested at the third- to fifth-grade reading level. She would tell them about the joy of reading, that it's more than pronouncing a bunch of words on paper. "You have to be able to comprehend what's in front of you and how to get from one place to another," she remembers telling her students.

She also schedules field trips to get them out of Binghampton, to show them there is life beyond the neighborhood.

The students are not bad children; they've just never had a solid foundation, the right discipline, the proper mentors. "We don't have enough in place to meet the children where they are," Clark-Nunley said. "If you have more mentors come in and help the kids and they see positive people, then they'll want to do different."

Penny's return to these courts was the talk of Binghampton, but it was in the halls and classrooms of Lester that teachers and administrators saw an even bigger impact. "When you're seeing Penny Hardaway up in your school in the Hood, you're always going to be surprised. But I began to see him over and over again," said Lester athletic director Demond Fason. "My first reaction was, He's for real."

Principal Antonio Burt added, "He's lived by a certain set of principles that his grandmother instilled in him. To this day, he still follows those principles. You have someone who is genuinely interested in the kids and his community. . . . The students are seeing him so much now, it's extra motivation for them to excel on all fronts. He comes to the school, checks on the kids. They see him as a face of stability—not someone who comes in, sells us a dream, and then a week or so later is gone. He lets them see: If you work hard, this is what you can have."

Clark-Nunley said she was in disbelief on many days because Penny was so punctual. She typically arrived at Lester at 7:15 A.M.; Penny would get there around seven in the morning. He walked the halls, visited classrooms, and asked teachers if they needed help—supplies, discipline, anything.

"It's unheard-of," Clark-Nunley said, "especially when he beats me to work in the morning. This is somebody who doesn't have to do anything, but he's there in the hallway."

As part of the team's disciplinary rules, Penny and Dez told teachers to notify them when their boys acted out of line. And there were plenty of times—players talking back to teachers, throwing food during lunch, skipping classes. The two coaches often would show up together. Other times, they would trade as to who would visit the classroom to talk with the student and teacher. Sometimes the entire coaching staff—Penny, Dez, the athletic director Fason, and Penny's cousin LaMarcus Golden—showed up. It was Penny's genuine interest in the children's lives that teachers found most inspiring. The other kids got jealous, but in a good way.

"When the kids looked up and saw who was walking in the door," Clark-Nunley said, "it was all attention where it needs to be. They understood there's going to be some consequences for this negative behavior."

"It wasn't a publicity stunt," Penny said. "I wanted to help Dez first of all, and come to help the kids, my school, my neighborhood. I wanted to let these kids know that I care, that I come from the same situation, and that they can make it, too. That was my purpose for coming back."

Andrew Murphy, one of two seventh graders on the team, lashed out at school—arguing with classmates, talking back to teachers, refusing to complete class assignments. An understandable reaction to his life being upended by his mother dying the year before. The death left him in the custody of his twenty-two-year-old sister, who was struggling herself and had just become pregnant. "It put the responsibility on his sister to raise him, and she's still a baby herself," Dez said.

"He's a good kid, but it's been really hard on him," Dez said. "He's got so much anger built up in him with not having his mom around. His mom was his life, and after she passed he didn't know what to do. In our community, we don't go to counseling and all that after deaths. We don't have the money for it. Really, you just gotta counsel yourself basically. The only way Andrew knew how to react was to be angry and take it out in everyday-life situations, as far as things in school."

Penny came to Nunley-Clark's classroom to speak with Andrew after he disrupted class. Penny talked with him about grief and dealing with loss. He spoke in a quiet voice, but the rest of the students could still hear his words. Nunley-Clark recalled that Penny told Andrew that his own mother abandoned him at an early age. His mother didn't die; she just up and left. "I had to take that, learn from it, pick it up, and move on," Penny told Andrew, as recalled by Nunley-Clark. "You have people here to support you in everything you do. They're your family now."

Penny and Dez decided the best way to help Andrew was to get him into a better living situation. Andrew moved in with Dez. "It ain't just about sports. It's about real life. After the game is over, you've still got to live your life," Dez said. As the season progressed, Andrew responded.

When Penny was notified that one of his sixth graders, Alex Lomax, fell asleep in class, he reported to the classroom within minutes. Penny told Alex about how he failed his senior year of high school and how it temporarily sidetracked his life.

"Don't you go down that same road," Penny said, according to Fason, who was present. "Stay focused."

The teachers knew to call Penny and Dez the moment there was a disruption from any of the players. Reggie and Robert weren't immune, either. "It was always something," Dez said, "somebody getting in trouble for things they had no business doing. I mean it was so much, you know, the stuff that kids do. Immature acts, not being disciplined.

"But Penny's not just looking at it from a far distance. He knows it from experience. That makes you be closer and have a relationship with everything in the whole community. He can relate to the kids' experience. He has a great sense of how they feel and what they're going through because he was one of these kids. Actually, he was all of these kids."

On one occasion, Robert walked out of his social studies class. Dez and Penny were summoned. When Robert saw the two of them, his shoulders hunched. He tried not to look them in the eyes. Penny told Robert his behavior was unacceptable, that he would apologize to the teacher and face more discipline at practice.

Another time, Penny addressed the entire sixth-grade class about growing up in the projects. He said he didn't always understand the lessons his grandmother preached when he was in his youth, but he was proud now of everything she taught him. He spoke of living the dream set forth by Martin Luther King Jr.

Don't let others destroy your dreams, he said.

Teachers saw attitudes change throughout the school. Kids would often stay late, work on assignments, and then head to the gym.

"Where you going?" Clark-Nunley would ask.

"We want to stick around to see Penny."

For teachers, it was the type of change kids at Lester had never seen. Many coaches expect teachers to let athletes slide. "It was special to actually have adults who cared and took the time out to mentor and monitor these kids, because that's what they need. They need structure," Clark-Nunley said. "Penny told them academics first, then athletics. And that was important for these kids to hear, because nobody told them that before."

College athletes sometimes get chided by the news media for seeking education degrees—that the curriculum is designed solely to pass football and basketball stars who have no plans ever to use the degree. In the halls of Lester, teachers witnessed Penny put his degree to work. "Look at how many athletes opt out of college," Clark-Nunley said. "They have the opportunity to go back, but they don't. But who did? Penny did."

Athletic director Fason said Penny gave "these kids a sense of *I can do it*. If the kids didn't believe before, they believe now.

"Desmond was like a big brother to the team, and Coach Hardaway came in and was like a father. The big brother is always getting on the kids, and the father is always directing them in the right direction. And that's what Coach Hardaway did. He showed them a life they've never imagined, having lived in the inner city of Binghampton all their lives. He became an inspiration to these kids. Prior to this year, they didn't want to come to school as quickly. But the two of them being involved, these young men wanted to be around something positive."

For the mother of Demarcus "Black" Martin it was welcome relief. Katictrese Taylor, thirty-four, was raising four children while struggling in the down economy, bills mounting every week. Black kept listening to his iPod during class. He argued with girls and got sent to detention regularly. "They helped by keeping his head on straight," she said. "I really appreciate everything Penny's doing for them, my son especially. He kept Demarcus focused."

Robert Washington's aunt Shree noticed her nephew's behavior shift into that of a more responsible young man. "When Penny stepped in, he kind of became a father role to him. He came in, picked him up, guided him in the right direction. He stayed on him when he was wrong, as far as the school lessons.

"I've seen a whole new Robert, a whole new smile. He came home and he used to talk about Penny and seeing Dez all the time," Auntie Shree continued. "I said, 'What's your daddy's name?' He said, 'Penny.' I said, 'Well, call your daddy up then!' He'd call and go over and spend the night at Penny's house. . . . I've never seen anything like it before. I've never had anybody from the NBA come show love to anyone in my family like he did and to these kids at the school."

Around the neighborhood, everyone pitched in—from teachers to gang members. Anything they could do to support the Lester Lions. Grandmas who couldn't attend games regularly because they didn't have cars found ways to get to the gym for tip-off. A couple of fathers who weren't active in the boys' lives showed up in the stands. Bozo Williams, the one who always pumped up the crowd, said Penny's presence got him to do something about his lifelong addiction to drugs. He went four months without using drugs.

"When you give up on yourself, you give up on life," he said. "So always believe in yourself."

Among the team's new fans was rapper MJG, the city's most famous hip-hop artist. In the song "Memphis," he immortalized life in his hometown Hood: *Getting fucked, getting money, pimpin' that's what we about.* MJG visited the team on several occasions during practice, sporting his long dreadlocks, flashy jewelry, and designer shades. He wanted the kids to know that image goes beyond outward looks. "You can look like me. You can dress like me, but you can still be a positive influence," MJG told me one afternoon at the Lester gym. "It's like the old saying: Feed a man a fish and he can eat for a day; but when you teach him to fish, he eats for life. All of this is building life skills.

"There's a lot of glamour and stuff in the Hood on the negative side," MJG said. "There's a lot of that type of stuff that the kids look up to. That's why it's always important to give that balance of other examples, of positive things. We can talk and we can jaw-jack, but at the end of the day it's all about helping and being a team and getting that victory. Learning to work together at a young age builds character."

And that, he said, was the takeaway from the team Penny and Desmond were building—teaching boys skills that would propel them to success off the court, telling the boys that they have a future in anything they want to pursue. It's important for a coach to connect with players, to get to know them as people and to tailor their coaching style to each individual. Penny knew the sensitivities of each player: Reggie's hurt from his father being locked up; Robert's need for gentleness because he was so sensitive; Andrew Murphy's pain from losing his mother.

In a neighborhood filled with squalor and bad examples, the importance of showing love to young teens began to make traction. Dez had introduced the concept in previous years. But Penny's presence and his devotion to strict rules took it to another level.

How the boys would respond remained the greatest question.

CHAPTER 10

Need for Discipline

Reggie Green cut toward the basket with the ball during practice. Kobe "the Mayor" Freeman reached in, stole it, and passed up court to Nick Merriweather, who immediately hit a three-pointer.

Penny yelled at Reggie, wanted to know what he was thinking. Reggie shook his head and flashed a look of anger. "You can leave if you want," Coach Penny barked.

Reggie peeled off his jersey and stormed out. Days earlier, Penny had lectured the team about staying united. He'd even mentioned that "all sorts of craziness" would hit the team on its quest to win state. And now Reggie was gone.

Reggie had begun rebelling in recent weeks. His home environment aside, he was upset Robert averaged more points than him—23 points a game to Reggie's 17. Reggie also didn't like the way Coach Penny disciplined him every time he messed up. But this time, Reggie committed the ultimate sin. He defied Coach in front of the entire team.

Penny gathered the remaining players and told them he expected Reggie to come back, but that quitting in the middle of practice was not the way to respond to pressure. It was unacceptable.

After practice, he and Coach Dez talked about punishment. Penny wanted to suspend Reggie for four games. But they decided to start with a one-game suspension and go from there. Reggie's response would ultimately decide the severity of his punishment.

When Reggie's grandfather caught wind of what happened, "I told him we're fixing to have a talk man-to-man," recalled Antoine Richardson.

"I told him I see your dad in you," Antoine said. "Boy, don't you be like that. You're gonna end up in trouble, you're gonna end up in jail. Don't be so vulgar and so mean to your teammates. And don't you ever quit. I know you're going through a lot, but carry your anger out on the other team. Please, listen to me, Reggie. Don't throw yourself around like you a bully because you think you're bigger than your teammates and your classmates. Yeah, you grew tall; yeah, you dunking the ball. That's good. But please— *please, Reggie*—don't throw your weight around. Your team needs you, and you need them!"

The Lester Lions suited up in their black and gold uniforms the next afternoon in the locker room. Reggie sat off to the side, in street clothes, his head slouched over.

Coach Dez liked to videotape the locker room before games— to analyze Penny's speeches and see how he could improve in his own speeches to the team. This time he pointed the camera at Reggie and zoomed in. "He got suspended for violating the team rules," Dez said.

Penny and Dez barred Reggie from sitting with the team on the bench. So he sat in the stands as Lester blew out Georgian Hill, a creampuff that didn't stand a chance even with Reggie suspended. Reggie had hoped to pad his stats against Georgian

Hill, to boost his 17 points a game average to around 20 points a game. Instead he watched Robert score bucket after bucket. It burned him up.

When fans saw Reggie in the bleachers, they peppered him with questions:

Why aren't you playing?

What did you do?

Why did you quit?

The questions only fueled his hunger. He wanted to be on the court bad. That was exactly what Penny and Dez hoped. Both coaches understood how much Reggie loved the game. By sitting him out, they knew it would build his character and he'd begin playing like a beast, playing up to his potential. The team improved to 14-3, but Penny knew they would need Reggie to complete their goal.

At practice the next day, Penny leaned against the yellow cinderblock wall in the locker room, the chalkboard next to him. He had grown tired of the team's selfishness. He wanted to reinforce that the infighting and ridiculous antics would not be tolerated. He was providing them an opportunity, an outlet to do great things, but it seemed they didn't appreciate anything.

"It's just like you're fighting your real brother or your real sister every single day," Penny said. "Would you fight your sisters every day, George? No, because you love them. Right? That's the same way I feel about y'all."

Love was not a word the boys heard enough of, especially from the black men of the neighborhood. It was a foreign concept to most—something that was completely lacking in their lives. Nine players sat on a wooden bench and the three others rested in plastic chairs, their eyes glued to Coach.

Penny was clear with Reggie that the weight of the team was on his shoulders.

"Being a leader is hard. For real. There aren't a lot of leaders in this world. I mean, there's not. Leadership is tough, because you can't just talk it; you've got to do it, too. That's what leaders do. Everybody wants to be the man. Everybody thinks they've got the game. But everybody's not a leader."

He scanned the players' faces. Penny had played with some of the greatest basketball players of all time: Magic Johnson, Michael Jordan, Charles Barkley, Shaq. Now here in Binghampton, the former face of Nike was preaching about the importance of staying true to oneself, of striving to be the best.

"Leadership is tough in all areas. In life. On the court." Penny had seen too many starters come to the sidelines and gripe after a sub went in. "When we take you out, you should be tired. You shouldn't be coming over to the bench saying, 'Man, I'm ready to go back' ten seconds later. That means you ain't doing what you're supposed to be doing on the court. The way we press, you're supposed to be so tired you want to come out. That's how it should be.

"But we're gonna keep coming the same way for the rest of this year, man. Because we have one goal. When I asked everybody who wanted to win state, everybody raised their hands. This is the time that's so important, putting in practice time."

If the team was going to complete the Run, it was time to get serious. Penny called out Reggie and Robert for being lazy practice players, guys who just wanted to score during games—for quitting. Such attitudes hurt the team camaraderie, and it prevented the coaching staff from introducing new plays. "I can't be putting it in," Penny said, "because I don't know if they're going to be game for wanting to do it. That's not picking on them, but that's how they are. They ain't practice players like that. They practice when they want to practice."

He started switching the practice teams up, pitting Reggie and Robert against each other to improve their competitive fire. When both players were on the same practice squad, the first team dominated the second team and "it was just starting to get boring.

"So we had to create some different ways. But, man, we just got to keep pushing forward."

Dez looked at Coach. Penny was about to bring down the hammer. They had gotten called to school after Black disrupted class and argued with a teacher. Other kids' classroom behavior was out of line. Robert was a practical joker who chatted in class, to the dismay of teachers. Separately, Kobe, Nick, and Black were summoned to the principal's office after they skipped a field trip and then conveniently met their classmates at a pizza joint.

"He knows all aren't going to make it pro, and he wants the best for them and they have to be prepared to live life beyond basketball," Dez recalled. "He knows what it takes to get them to the point where they need to be at in life."

Penny was in no mood for jokes in that locker room. It was one thing to goof around in practice, but disrespecting teachers would not be tolerated.

"Everybody understands you can't be in class just doing what you want to do. I mean, the teachers are not going to go for it, and everything's going to get back to Coach Dez. When they have to call him up to the school, that's the last thing you want," he said. "Well, we're going to have to pay for it."

He explained how Coach Dez used to keep players out for a quarter or two for bad behavior. Penny shook his head. "It's still rewarding you to play when you do something like that. If you feel like you're getting rewarded anyway if you do wrong, you're going to keep doing wrong."

Penny let the players absorb his words.

"I don't believe in that. If you're going to do something real disrespectful, you don't deserve to play in the game. That way, you will know not to do it the next time. Somebody else will go ahead and play. That's just how it works."

Penny tossed it over to Coach Dez. "You got anything else, Coach?"

"That's just what it is," Dez said. "That's it."

Four or five players stood up and began stretching.

Penny wasn't finished. He said they would be running extra stairs and sprints this day, because he was tired of their disrespect.

"It's not funny no more," he said.

"People want to be cutting up in class. People want to be quitting on the team. People want to do what they want to do. We're supposed to be a family," Penny said. "We ain't supposed to be like that! The only reason we have to do this is because if we don't, you're going to keep doing it. That's a reflection on your family, on the school, on the community, and on us—and on yourself. We can't keep letting you do that."

He went down the line—Courtney, Black, Alex, Andrew, Derrick, Nick, Xavier, Robert, Kobe. He allowed them an opportunity to air their thoughts.

"Anybody here got something to say? Because right now is the time to talk. We don't feel like we're right about everything, but on discipline I said that when I first got here: We're not going to shortcut on discipline. We ain't gonna do you wrong, but y'all ain't gonna do us wrong, either."

The team grew silent.

Penny got to the last player.

"Reggie?" Penny asked.

A grumble could be heard.

"Hold on, Reggie's got something to say."

Reggie sat crouched in a yellow plastic chair, his head facing down. Dressed in a white T-shirt and black basketball shorts, he turned his head to look at Penny.

"I want to apologize for how I acted at practice the other day," he said. "I had walked out and I had got mad. I don't know what was wrong with me. I just want to let y'all know I apologize and let you know that they don't deserve to run."

Penny wasn't going to let the apology go unnoticed. His voice picked up a notch. "That takes a real man to apologize. For real. When somebody doesn't apologize, that's when you can just go about your business. But apologizing means a lot. It means you do care. That's what we want you to do. We want you to mean it."

Penny said Reggie was one of the few players in the nation who could carry the entire team on his back toward a title. "That's a lot of pressure on you. But if you come out there with energy and playing the way we know you can play, we win the state easy.

"Who can say that in the country? That we can win state if just one dude comes and plays hard. Not just play, but play hard.

That's how much talent he has and that's how much he can dominate the game on both ends of the floor."

Reggie flashed his million-dollar smile and squirmed in his chair, almost uncomfortable at the praise being heaped his way.

"We accept the apology," Penny said. "But them jokers are still running because of Black."

Penny turned toward Demarcus, aka Black. "We got another situation," Penny said. "You can't be talking in class, talking to the teacher like you're crazy or whatever. We're not going to have that. Nope. There's gotta be discipline.

"You know what everybody thinks about Lester, man? Everybody thinks Lester is just a school that's full of a bunch of Hood kids that don't know what they're doing—that all they want to do is fight, all they want to do is get in trouble.

"Don't nobody want their kid to transfer to Lester, because they think their kid is going to decline. That's the mentality that they have. Why do we keep giving them that?"

Penny motioned to the coaching staff. Lester athletic director Demond Fason had walked into the locker room.

"I'm a product of Binghampton," Penny said. "Dez is a product of Binghampton. He went to college. I went to college and graduated. LaMarcus went to college. Coach Fason went to college, right?"

"Of course," said Coach Fason, laughing. "I'm a product of Binghampton, too, Coach."

Drawing his speech to a close, Penny said, "We gotta shed this image of what Binghampton is. For real."

The next afternoon, Lester played at the Memphis Academy of Science and Engineering. Known as MASE, the school was best known for producing young scientists, not basketball players. The school's motto: "Excellence Without Excuses."

There were no excuses this day. The scientists got crushed, like they'd been put in an atom smasher. The Lions built a 28–9 half-time lead and cruised the rest of the way to a 54–14 win. Reggie was allowed to play limited time after his apology.

"I really appreciated him doing that because he was the captain of the team," Penny said. "By him quitting, he didn't lead by example. By him apologizing, that's what a man stands for. You're going to make mistakes in life. Just come back and apologize for it."

Another chink in the armor came two days after the victory at MASE. It was Robert's turn to walk out on the team, again. He just didn't feel like running. Robert's mother walked him back to the gym and spoke with Coach Dez. Penny had gone on a business trip that day. He missed the day's antics, but he and Dez spoke for an hour by phone on how best to handle the situation.

If Robert was testing Dez with Penny gone for the day, he was in for a rude awakening. Dez was angry and frustrated. He wasn't going to be seen as a pushover. He dressed down Robert in front of the whole team. "He'd rather play for the damn community center than for the school. I'm talking what kind of sense does that make?" Dez told the team.

Robert, he said, was a "seller," a Hood term for somebody who "just thinks they can do anything."

"He don't even care about his momma, sisters, brothers, his aunties. Nothing.

"If he did, he'd have been here today. Why does his momma gotta bring him back to practice?" Dez said. "That shows you the type of person he is. Your momma's gotta bring you back to practice?"

Robert sat expressionless. The other boys didn't utter a word.

"For real, he don't care. He's heartless. He don't care about none of y'all. You think he's your friend, but he's really not. He's just laughing and giggling with you. But later on in life, as you get older, when it's time to go to high school and all that stuff, just watch the man he becomes if he don't get his mind right."

Dez spoke of another Binghampton legend named Ricky Hearn, a 6-foot-6 do-it-all guard whom Antoine Richardson and Penny had tried to help a few years before. Ricky went to prep school and got kicked out for getting his nose stuck in cocaine. He was provided a second chance, at a junior college in West Virginia, where his addiction grew. He now stands as a sad example of wasted talent.

"Ricky could've been playing in the NBA right now. He had the height, the skills, the shooting. He had everything and look at how he turned out," Dez told the players. "That's Robert."

Ricky could do anything on the basketball court, Dez said, but his "mind wasn't right. He let this neighborhood suck him in, and that's not a good thing.

"Binghampton is just like a pit. You can easily get sucked into all the bad things that go on in this neighborhood. I'm talking about like ninety percent of the people over here had all the talent in the world, but they won't allow themselves to be better than what they're doing.

"Penny's the only one that allowed himself to be better. Y'all should be very appreciative, but you don't even understand. For real. That man walked the same streets you walked. He walked through the same field in Howze Park. And just look at him. Do you understand how much he is worth? . . . There's twelve or thirteen people in here, and you don't even understand you're around a dude that has made over two hundred million dollars."

Not a single kid showed any sign of surprise. Dez would've gotten a bigger response if he said Penny made a thousand dollars. Dez noticed the lack of reaction and chided them. "Y'all can't even count that high.

"He's the richest black person to ever come out of Memphis in history," Dez said. "Just think about that in this small little city, and he's amongst you right now. He's up here every day giving it his all. He spends his time over here, and he doesn't have to do anything.

"I remember the first time he called me. He was like 'What type of team do you have?' I said just come on over here and see for yourself. You might like them, but I don't know if you will. But from that first day, he loved these two dudes right here."

Dez motioned to Reggie and Robert, the team's two star quitters. "Penny ain't never gonna let anything happen to anyone in here. But you don't even give your hearts, especially you two," Dez said.

Reggie and Robert had slacked off again in practice. While the rest of the team ran sprints as hard as they could, the two lagged behind, barely putting in any effort, as if they were better than everyone else, as if they played by another set of rules. "You only care about yourself," Dez said. "It ain't nobody's fault but yours.

"You think you're pretty, because these little nappy-headed girls like y'all. Man, those girls ain't shit. Look, girls are gonna be here for the rest of your life. Believe me, I know for a fact, when you're doing good, they're always going to love you. For real. Just wait, you will see. Wait till you get hurt or miss a couple games. They'll move down the bench."

The players giggled with laughter, the first sign they were listening. Girls, Dez said, "change just like the weather."

Penny provided shoes, uniforms, financial support, and academic help to everyone on the team. Didn't the kids understand what kind of prize they had been given?

"That man is pouring his heart out," Dez said, "but y'all will mess up a wet dream."

In the locker room, Dez changed the subject to Lester's most recent game, the 54–14 thrashing of MASE. The first time the teams played, Lester kept MASE to 7 points. This time, MASE doubled their total. "That means y'all ain't playing no defense," Dez said.

Their rival Hamilton, he said, was already talking about beating Lester in the city playoffs. To counter that trash talk, Dez said the team needed to focus. He wrote "DISCIPLINE" across the chalkboard.

"We've got to start going hard the whole game," Dez said. "We've got to get back to what we've been doing: playing hard defense, scrapping and scoring layups, and making smart decisions."

Penny reinforced that point after several days of intense conditioning drills. He too wrote "DISCIPLINE" on the chalkboard. He underlined it twice.

"This is the number-one thing," Penny said. "This isn't just a negative thing as far as torturing or punishing somebody. All the great teams talk about it: discipline on offense; discipline on defense."

He apologized to Reggie, saying he hadn't been getting enough scoring opportunities. "I look at your size, your athleticism. You should dominate the game. But we haven't put you in a position to dominate the game." Penny drew up a couple of quick plays to get the ball in Reggie's hands on fast breaks. He told Reggie and Robert to stop arguing with the guards.

"We're gonna have to start making these teams pay," he said.

Toward the end of the speech, he circled "DISCIPLINE." "We're working hard and playing hard. But the discipline and the smart play just is not there."

"When we play a tough team"—Penny paused and mentioned Fayette East specifically—"it's going to be way tougher because those teams are disciplined in their game planning. That's just how it is."

The next afternoon, Lester traveled to Treadwell, the nearby Memphis high school where Penny rose to stardom. Treadwell is home to another star Memphian, wrestling legend Jerry "the King" Lawler. Now a middle school, Treadwell was overwhelmed like Andy Kaufman in the ring with Lawler. The Lions pile-drived Treadwell, 74–20.

The Run was in full effect.

Lester entered the final game of the season with a 16-3 record and a five-game winning streak.

But nothing was guaranteed.

CHAPTER 11

Truce

The GDs, Vice Lords, Bloods, and Crips have been rooted in Memphis nearly as long as FedEx. The GDs were the first to arrive in big numbers in the 1980s, moving in from Chicago during the crack epidemic. The others soon followed, bringing with them a wave of violence: drug trafficking, pimping, robbing, shootings, rapes. They staked out turf and rivalries formed. Around the city, the six-point star of the GDs is painted on abandoned buildings. Stop signs are tagged with "CK," for "Crip Killer," by the Bloods. The Crips will mark their territory with the three-point crown. Vice Lords will use a five-point star. To disrespect the GDs, they'll spray paint an upside-down pitchfork.

Kids as young as ten years old join gangs, in some cases even younger. They enter gangs for an array of reasons: peer pressure, elevated status, intimidation. In the months since I first began visiting Memphis, at least three East High School students were killed in random gang violence. "You've got a lot of young kids— ages nine to seventeen—with guns shooting over anything," said Ray Lepone, a Shelby County prosecutor who heads a gang and narcotics unit.

Over lunch one afternoon I sat across from Black Ice (his gang name) at Perkins on Poplar to learn more about why kids join gangs.

"I got in for the fun of it. I didn't know what I was doing," said Black Ice.

He joined a gang in a bathroom in an elementary school in the Hollywood neighborhood of North Memphis. It didn't seem like much. "A friend said, 'We're big dogs.' It wasn't like a sacrifice to get in where you get jumped. It wasn't like nowadays where there's initiation and all that. It was kind of like the thing to do, but it was the wrong thing to do."

More than thirty years later, that choice still haunts him. "Once you're in, you're in. There ain't no turning back." At 6-feet-5, he could crush anyone with his giant fists, but he says he stays mostly in his house playing video games these days to avoid getting shot or mugged or put in a situation where bad shit goes down.

"I got with the wrong crowd," he said. "If I stayed with the right crowd, I think I could've gone on, gotten out of Memphis and played basketball in college and gotten a degree. I think I'd be doing something positive to this day."

Although he is only in his late thirties, he is already the father of four boys and four girls. "I talk to them every day about the situation I chose. I chose the wrong path, and I tell them that. I started selling drugs, and I tell them just try to keep your heads above your shoulders."

He lets me in on insights of gang life. It's not exciting or cool. Far from it. Betraying a gang leader gets you "6 Minutes No Coverup," when fists pound your face like Rocky Balboa in a slaughterhouse. "You can't move, you can't flinch. You've got to stand there and take the six minutes like a man," Black Ice said. "That's how we got punished." The violations can be for anything from fighting fellow gang members to robbing someone within the gang to disrespecting someone.

A few months earlier he came across a gang member who had robbed him of twenty thousand dollars in cash in a drug deal gone wrong in New York. "When I saw him, the first thing I thought is: I'm fixing to get you." He contemplated the consequences of what that would mean, especially for his children. "I thought about it, but decided it's a lost situation. It's a lost thing," he said. "You learn from life."

Benevolence is not something you hear much about when it comes to gangs. But winning changes everything. With the Lester Lions on a roll, the Binghampton gangs actually started acting as school crossing guards. They hosted team barbecues. Some showed up at practice and worked with Reggie and Robert on post moves.

The cynical assessment would be that the gangs were interested in getting a piece of the action. If the next Penny Hardaway emerged from Binghampton, they wanted the players to owe them something or at the very least to respect them.

But there was also a great amount of respect on the street for Penny and Dez.

"It's getting known on the streets that they're trying to make a positive thing out of everything," Black Ice said. "They're motivating young black kids who ain't got parents, who don't have places to stay every night, who don't have food to eat. Penny's taking them in like sisters and brothers. And Penny's taking them in the right way.

"Anytime you're trying to get some young black kids to do the right thing, it's always a good thing. Most of us always end up on the wrong side of the track or in jail with life sentences."

He said he preaches to his own children that the day may come "when I may not be here for you." Along with that sober message, he tells them to "stay away from guns, drugs, gangs. I just tell them, 'Stay on the right ship.'"

Penny and Dez righted the ship by talking with rival gangs about calming tensions, about setting aside allegiances. There wasn't an actual powwow where GDs, Vice Lords, Bloods, and Crips sat down and sang "Kumbaya." It originated out of loyalty to old friends. On these streets, there's a thin line between those who join gangs and those who are clean. Long before initiations and bandannas, they were friends. And so Dez and Penny talked with them, not as enemies, but as friends.

In Binghampton, the black and gold stood for Lester, not the Vice Lords. And, amazingly, the gangs listened. I'm told there was a truce agreed upon during the basketball season.

"I don't think of them as gang members," Coach Dez said. "I look at them as my brothers. Penny and I and those who are affiliated with gangs, we grew up together. So we can go to them and talk to them about anything. . . . Once you get into the core of Binghampton, you get mad love from the people who are supposed to be the 'bad guys'—because they see the light, too, that helping these kids is our future. It will instill something in the kids to do better than the previous generation. And that'll make the community better as a whole.

"We always get the negative press . . . because that's always been what Binghampton is known for: causing trouble and robbing and killing."

LaMarcus Golden, Penny's cousin and assistant coach, said, "If the gang members see the neighborhood and these kids are getting good, positive attention, you feel like a little later on that it might inspire some of these older guys to get a job or to do things in the neighborhood that are positive. They understood that and made an impact, instead of trying to do it in their own way of selling drugs and settling things with violence."

In an ideal world, gangs wouldn't be part of the community, but in Binghampton it is an inescapable reality—this is where they live and you can't ignore the gang presence. And as horrible as the gang activity may be, the members still found pride in achievement. They identified with Penny because he's a winner. By him returning to Beautiful Black Binghampton, he brought a new sense of what it meant to be from BBB.

And whatever bad choices the gang members made in their lives, this time they made a right choice by helping the children.

I had heard the word *truce* a few times, but I couldn't help but wonder if it was just wishful thinking or spin. Gangs helping middle school kids instead of preying on them? There's a saying in journalism: If the story sounds too good to be true, it usually is. And so I found myself standing outside the Lester Community Center talking with two men who I was told were Binghampton gang leaders. One with the street name of Love, aged twenty-five, had the stereotypical Hollywood gangster look: gold teeth, necklaces, and tattoos. His forehead might as well have said, "Don't Fuck With Me." The other, identified as God, looked just the opposite: clean-cut in a polo shirt. At twenty-eight, God more resembled a frat boy.

I was an interloper, an obvious trespasser. A couple of nights earlier in a black-only nightclub where rock—*and I don't mean the pea gravel type*—was passed around like Bud Light, I was in the bathroom when a dude approached. "You from Germantown," he sneered, a reference to the wealthiest white suburb. I flinched and waited for my face to get smashed in when I responded with "Hell, naw, I'm from the BBB—Beautiful Black Binghampton." Somehow the guy found my answer satisfactory.

I had that same initial uneasy feeling with Love and God. I was on their turf, after all. I greeted them with the Binghampton "One Love" handshake, a move that prompted cackles of laughter. We exchanged pleasantries. I told them I appreciated the neighborhood welcoming me, a white dude from the East Side.

"You get to see our heart," Love said. "The season kind of tells our story in Binghampton. We've been down for so many years. Now we have time to turn tragedy into triumph."

The lessons that Penny and Dez imparted on the kids of Lester, the two explained, are not lost on them and their members. The gangs have talked with the children of the neighborhood "to stay positive and stay on the right path."

"We tell them, 'Don't do nothing bad,'" said God. "Don't go negative."

Added Love, "Desmond and Penny are helping guide the kids right."

I asked if it was really true that the neighborhood gangs were in full agreement, that they weren't to lay their hands on the boys of Lester. "It's hands off kids, period," Love said. "We don't get involved like that. Dez and Penny are coaching and doing something positive. What they're doing on the court with the basketball situation, that can translate to life as well."

"Dez, he came all the way back from everything he went through with cancer. And he's come back strong, and he's giving us love," God said.

"He's fighting with us," Love added. "He's giving us something to fight for, like hope. You know, we're down. We're going through everything—poverty and all—but we're still here and we're still fighting."

God: "It ain't bad as it seems. Everybody's like one big family.

We all look out for everyone's kids. It's really like we're always looking out for each other."

The two gang leaders blamed the media for focusing too much on violence and for glamorizing gangs on TV. I wondered if this was a new low for journalists, even gang leaders harping about negative news coverage.

"The truth of it is it's going to be a little too boring," Love said. "So they gotta spice it up, add a little flavor, just to make it a little more than what it is.

"All the negative things get a light shined on it," he continued. "But all the positive things, they never shine a light on it. There's a lot of positive things going on but the press don't print that."

Both talked of the Lester Street murders—when six people, including a two-year-old, were killed in a Binghampton home in March 2008—an act so heinous it disgusts even them. They're angry because the killings were so gruesome they hijacked the name of Lester Middle School. The rest of Memphis associated the name Lester with the murder rampage.

"It happened in Binghampton, but it was on down the road. But it gave the whole neighborhood a lot of negative publicity, like we're crazy. We would never let nothing happen to kids like that," said Love.

"It gave us a bad look, a bad image," added God.

Worse yet, the two explained, the killer was from a different neighborhood. Gangs don't like it when an outsider comes into their "house" and causes problems. The Lester Street killer had roots from outside Binghampton, but his actions cast a pall over their neighborhood.

"We ain't never know him, but that made the whole neighborhood look bad," Love said. "But looka here, Penny and Dez are doing something good. So we gotta support something positive. We've just gotta hold it up and be proud of it."

"Everything happens for a reason," God said. "That's the way I look at it."

"We don't want the kids to fall to the streets," Love continued. "That's why we're trying to guide them, point them in the right direction. Let them know there are other things you can do—that there's a whole world out there."

"It's a bigger and better world out there," said God. "It might be harder from where we come from. They might have to put more energy and pressure into succeeding to help get where they need to go, because we don't have it like everybody else."

"We've got to give them more heart and feeling," Love said.

"And give them opportunities to do more things," God said.

"When we do something for the kids, it's from the heart," Love continued. "We want to see them do better. We want to better our community. We're trying to turn Binghampton into Binghampton the Beautiful."

"We want a new generation, a better generation to come through here," God said. "For our kids to get out, we have an extra struggle. So we try to keep the kids positive, keep their pride up. They're making us look good, even though we might never have had a chance."

They admitted there are limits. "We're trying to protect the neighborhood from outsiders trying to move into the neighborhood and mess it up," Love said. "Every man's gotta protect their family. You can't let nothing happen to nobody. But at the same time, we're trying to do something positive."

I mentioned how my white friends in Memphis feared I would be jacked up in Binghampton. Love said that's the image they're trying to change. "Like your friends say, they feel as if everything out here is treacherous, terrorist—that something is going to happen to you. So when people come out here, they're already on the defensive. It ain't like that. We're trying to unify."

Love and God were just boys when Penny was in his prime. The NBA all-star brought hope when they were growing up, and he's doing it again by coming back to coach. Never have they seen a uniting force like this.

"I like the fact Penny came back to the neighborhood," Love said. "We've been trying to do this in the neighborhood for a while, but it was harder to get the vision together. You know what I'm saying? When he came back, he gave everybody spirit, like we can do it. Then all of a sudden, it's giving us a reason to celebrate, a reason to remain kosher and calm and just celebrate and unite."

I spoke later with Lester athletic director Demond Fason about this phenomenon. He put it this way. "It goes to show you that even though a person might be doing something negative, they also respect positive. The gang members were some of our biggest supporters," he said. "It's amazing."

Across town, U.S. Attorney Ed Stanton formed a multi-agency gang unit in what has become the largest war on gangs in Tennessee history. He wants the hit men, the coke dealers, the killers, the rapists running roughshod over the city thrown in prison without the opportunity for parole. Stanton is a black Memphian who grew up in the dangerous South Side, where "people were selling drugs and getting into nefarious activities." Some of his friends ended up in jail; others faced "even more severe circumstances."

Stanton attended Memphis State at the same time as Penny. The two even shared a biology class; the first ten minutes of class began with the professor talking about the most recent Tiger game with Penny. The first member of his family to graduate from college, Stanton went on to law school and eventually rose to become senior counsel for FedEx. "Two different tracks, two different trajectories, but we're two fortunate ones," Stanton said of Penny and himself.

His gang crackdown covers twenty-two counties in west Tennessee, an area spanning from the Tennessee River to the Mississippi River. Memphis is the hub and spoke of gang activity, but the gangs have spread into the eastern suburbs and into rural communities where local cops are outnumbered and outgunned in the burgeoning meth and prescription pill drug trade. The suburb of Covington has become known as Little Memphis.

The reason for the growth is wide-ranging. When Memphis projects—havens for drug dealers and pimps and gangbangers— were torn down, it flushed gangsters into the outlying areas. Troubled kids from cities like Chicago and East St. Louis get sent south to stay with relatives. Gangs also have realized that the rural communities have few law enforcement officers and a high profit on the drug trade. Trafficking of women and girls is on the rise, too.

"We have seen very real and serious elements of gangs" in rural areas, Stanton said. "This is not something that's a folk tale. This is something that's real."

Another alarming trend is the tendency of gangs to recruit, and not just the kids dropping out of school. They're "more savvy now, recruiting individuals that are smart, that have high GPAs, that don't look like your average gang member. We've seen honor roll students claiming to be part of gangs."

"A lot of times it seems glamorous to the young guys. They're enamored by what they see on TV and in videos," Stanton said. "But to see what it takes to get out of one of these gangs and what you're signing up for, oftentimes they don't know. So if we can reach that boy or girl before they decide to cross that line and enter into a gang, the better our community will be."

He doesn't know if there are measurable statistics on whether crime went down in Binghampton during the season. But the mere fact gangs agreed to support the kids, instead of killing them, is reason for applause.

While Stanton is focused on locking up the most violent offenders and destroying the gangs' enterprise, he said, "We're fooling ourselves if we think we can arrest our way out of the gang element here in this community. It's going to take an equal commitment from the stakeholders in the community. When you have somebody like a Penny Hardaway and others pitching in and doing what they're doing, it makes a tremendous difference."

CHAPTER 12

Know Your Friends

When Penny was a freshman in college, having missed the basketball season due to academic ineligibility, he would often go to a local Memphis gym to practice. He was on his way back from there one Sunday night late in April 1991 and headed to his cousin LaMarcus Golden's when he almost became a statistic of Memphis violence. LaMarcus lived with his parents in a gang-infested area in North Memphis where drug deals and shootings were so frequent "you got used to hearing gunshots and police and ambulance sirens."

"When I was young, the gangs were so bad, when it got dark, you couldn't be outside," LaMarcus recalled. "If they saw you out, they would do something to you."

It was about 9:30 P.M. when Penny and his longtime friend Terry Starks pulled up. They waited in Starks's SUV at the curb while Penny tried to reach LaMarcus on the phone. He was trying to return LaMarcus's wallet, which had been left accidentally at the gym. A beige old-school Cadillac circled the block with four men inside. "I look back and see the same car turning around in the driveway three homes behind us. It pulls out, comes by us, and goes on down again," Penny recounted. "But this time, I'm still not catching on as to what's going on. But I'm getting skeptical."

His friend went to the back of his SUV and opened the hatch to get LaMarcus's wallet. The Caddy slowed.

"Hey, man, can you tell me how to get to Bartlett?" the driver asked.

Bartlett was a nice suburban area, far from the Memphis inner city. Penny knew that question was code for *Your ass is about to get jacked up.*

"At that moment, everything clicked," Penny said. "I thought, Oh, man."

Penny, nineteen, had a gun shoved in his face and he was soon facedown on the wet pavement. Starks also was forced to the ground in the middle of the street, a gun drawn on him, too. "I kept thinking, He's going to shoot me in my back, he's going to shoot me in my head," Penny told the *Commercial Appeal* at the time.

The gangsters stole Penny's necklace, watch, ring, and gym bag. Starks was robbed of money and his shoes.

As the Caddy sped away, three gunshots rang out. Penny ducked behind the SUV. He thought about hitting the pavement, but instead jumped inside the cargo area. A pain rocketed through his foot.

"I told my friend, 'I've been hit.'"

He took off his shoe. His sock was bloodied. Three metatarsals in his right foot were broken. The bullet remained lodged in his foot for several months, because doctors feared removing it would cause nerve damage. "He was very fortunate," Memphis State trainer Eddie Cantler told the local paper.

The bullet had ricocheted off the ground, preventing a direct hit. "It ricocheted right where I thought about diving on the pavement. If I would have done that, I would have been hit in the head," Penny said at the time.

"The Good Lord was with Anfernee on this one," Memphis State coach Larry Finch said.

Penny would defy the anti-snitching street code. He went to police headquarters and picked out those responsible. The shooter never gave up the gang life. He remains imprisoned on drug charges and other felony offenses. "When somebody shoots you from another neighborhood, you don't hesitate. I'm a basketball player. I'm not a gangster," Penny said. "I knew I was doing the right thing."

But the shooting made news for other reasons, too.

Starks, the thirty-two-year-old friend, had been indicted by a federal grand jury just months before in 1990 on a charge of distributing cocaine. He was awaiting trial. Starks was the president of MegaJam Records in Memphis and had been busted in a hotel with $226,000 cash in his possession and a kilo of cocaine with an estimated street value of $700,000. He eventually pleaded guilty and was sentenced to five years in prison, which he did serve.

Penny said Starks was a lifelong friend and that he knew nothing of his drug involvement. "I've grown up knowing Terry, and he'll always be a friend of mine," Penny told the *Commercial Appeal* a couple of months after the incident. "But it bothered me. Some people projected me as a dope dealer because the newspaper talked about Terry."

Coach Finch spoke with Penny about choosing friends more wisely. "My kids have to distinguish a person's character," Finch said. "Every time one of my kids talks to somebody, I don't have time to run a character check."

Penny would always look back on that day.

"I think about, man, what would've happened if I got hit some-where else," he told me. "I could've passed away, I could've been paralyzed. Anything could've happened. So I'm definitely thank-ful for not being put in a situation where I was shot on sight and killed."

But the biggest lesson learned: "It taught me not to be naïve."

CHAPTER 13

Homecoming

The payoff that Penny and Coach Dez had almost given up on came in the week of homecoming. The team had improved to 16-3, but it was a different record that most impressed the coaches, when the players entered the gym with their progress reports. "Every one of them was better," Penny recalled. "Guys went from D's and C's to A's and B's. Some went from F's to B's. I was really proud of them for that. Some went to mandatory tutorial sessions. Those who didn't need it stayed in the right area or got better. They all got motivated.

"When people in Memphis think about Lester, they think: I don't want my kids going there. There's a bunch of guys doing the wrong things. That's not what we have. We have some really good kids who need focus and mentors."

In Reggie Green's living room, his grandma displayed a simple sheet designating his place on Lester's honor roll with a 3.7 GPA. "He's a good boy. That's my boy," said Sheila Harris. "I'm proud of him. Maybe one day we will come up outta the ghetto. That's all I got to say: Maybe one day we will come up outta the ghetto. . . . I tell Reggie, 'Just because we stay here, don't mean we got to act like we're from here.'"

Robert Washington's grades rose from C's and D's to a 2.9 GPA, the most improved student in the school, according to athletic director Fason. Reading teacher Monica Clark-Nunley said her favorite moment was seeing Robert get honored by the school counselor in front of the entire student body. He walked hunched over in his humble aw-shucks manner. "That was a spark that really got him motivated," the teacher said.

Robert's aunt Shree said she now had higher ambitions for Robert. "I want to see him finish school—graduate high school for sure and follow in Penny's footsteps: Go aim for the best. We stay in the Hood. Like I told Robert and all my nieces and nephews: It's great for somebody from the NBA to come back and show you love and walk in the way that he walks. I mean, what else could you ask for?"

Penny's cousin LaMarcus said the improved grades and the truce among the neighborhood gangs were two of the most spectacular things he ever observed. "We were trying to show the kids that they need positive attention. Some of the guys were thinking about going down the wrong path and choosing that direction. We just tried to teach these kids that with education and hard work, you have a future."

There was no way Lester would lose homecoming and their last regular season game. At school, more than five hundred students packed the auditorium for a pep rally to further pump up the team. Onstage, rappers busted a specially made rhyme, what had become the team's fight song:

King of the jungle
Yeah, I'm a Lion
Super fly swag
You can say my flag's flying

A couple of hours later, the players dressed in their Sunday best. Penny had taken the team on a shopping spree to Macy's so they would look dapper for this moment. About fifteen hundred people crammed into the Lester gym to see the team finish the regular season. The gym was so packed, fans lined up two deep along the baseline. Antoine Richardson found a seat behind the bench. Reggie's grandma joined the crowd. Robert's aunt Shree, grandmother, mom, and uncles sat in the bleachers.

Bozo Williams raised his arms to entice the crowd into rowdy cheers. He once again twisted his body to spell the school name. The crowd roared louder with each letter. The place was bumping and grinding.

"L-E-S-T-E-R!"

Inside the locker room, the players tried to block out the commotion in the gym. They spoke with a camera crew about Penny's transformative power, outside of his presence. Reggie said he had never known how good Penny was until he went on YouTube and saw highlights and "I saw them shoes."

Kobe said "it makes you feel great" when your coach has starred in the NBA and became the face of Nike. "Every middle school team would like an NBA player to be their coach, but we got lucky," Kobe said.

He said he would be moving on to high school next year but would succeed because of Penny's discipline. No matter what, Kobe said, he would "stay humble and never get the big head.

"I ain't looking forward to next year right now," he added. "I'm staying here with my family, right now."

The players thanked Penny for uniforms, for their Foamposite shoes, for taking them out to eat, for providing their families with money to get by on a daily basis. Every player said they hoped to go to college and eventually play basketball professionally. Nick Merriweather said he hoped to become a Hollywood producer; one said he wanted to become a doctor.

Guard Demarcus "Black" Martin pretends to bowl as his teammates act like bowling pins—a sign of the camaraderie the team developed over the course of the season.

Most said they had struggled to eat meals regularly, but Penny changed that. "I've been getting a lot of love from him, like joyful," Kobe said. "Anybody like that . . ." He paused to gather his thoughts. "We just got a lot of respect for him, because he ain't got to do this."

Reggie flashed a grin from ear to ear. "I appreciate him a lot," he said. "I appreciate all the things he's done. He taught us to be disciplined and he taught us how to play the game. We're still learning. I appreciate him helping me on my big-man skills and telling me to play smart during the games. . . . He gives us anything we need, and I just want to say thank you for doing all that."

Andrew Murphy, whose mother had died, agreed. "I want to thank Penny for not only helping us with the basketball but our life. He don't have to get involved with it." He repeated, "He doesn't have to be over here pushing us, but he do. I just want to thank him for all that."

"He buys us shoes and gives us life lessons with all of the stuff that he has done," Courtney McLemore said. "He ain't have to be here doing it with us, but he do it because he chooses to do it."

"I want to tell Penny I love him," Kobe added, "and the rest of us love him."

Nick Merriweather, the tiny warrior who had seen his father go through so much battling cancer, simply thanked Coach Penny for "life lessons." He didn't need to say anything more. Penny "taught us to be a better person," added Derrick Carnes. "I thank him for being a role model in our life. He treats us like we're his own kids."

"I just want to thank Penny because he came here and helped me out and treated me like his son," Robert said. "I love him."

A knock on the door interrupted the taping. It was Coach Penny. The mood in the gym was electric: bass-thumping music, guys with extra struts, moms with wide smiles. The players could hear the fans pulsating, their chants, their rhythmic clapping. Penny was excited, too, but first he had to address a situation. Demarcus had gotten in trouble for arguing with a girl who had swiped at him and for listening to an iPod in class. Penny spoke privately with Demarcus about the need to control his temper, but now Coach called him out in front of the team.

"You're going to miss your day because somebody hit you? I mean, come on. You've got to be smarter than that.

"We're not at the point where you can disrespect teachers or other people. If somebody does something to you, you don't have to react," he said. "There's going to be a lot of people do a lot of things to you guys in life—that doesn't mean you react every time. It don't mean that. See y'all get mad and you just lose it. You can't lose it in every situation. Sometimes you've just got to be a bigger person and be like, 'Aiight, I'll just go tell the teacher to get my stuff back.'

"When y'all get in trouble, we said the discipline is just that. There ain't no excuse. No excuse!" He rolled his head in exasperation. "We'll just have to deal with it after today. But today, the eighth graders, enjoy the day. Today's your day. You'll never get this again."

In the gym, a walkway of yellow and black balloons lined the middle of the floor. Each player was introduced to the enthusiastic squeals of the crowd and awarded trophies. When the pomp and circumstance was finished, there was basketball to be played.

Dez always collected the uniforms at the end of games and washed them. He reached into his bag and handed out jerseys and shorts. "The game hasn't even started, and it's already over," Dez quipped.

The victim this evening was the Cummings School, a city school with a focus on enriched academics. Basketball was not the Eagles' specialty. The Lions nearly shut out Cummings in the 59–7 homecoming victory. At one point Reggie broke free and took off from just under the free throw line for a thunderous dunk that brought Binghampton to its feet. He blew kisses to his grandmother. He'd been dunking since seventh grade; they'd just grown more elaborate this season. In blowouts, Penny would leave Reggie in the game until he got his breakaway dunk. Then Penny would yank the starters.

It was the perfect cap to the season.

The words of Penny's grandmother from so many years earlier rang true: "Do for your community, do for your people, do what God puts in your heart." He and Dez had weathered turmoil, in-fighting, and selfishness. Penny had learned that giving money to the school and community over the years wasn't good enough. "What they really needed was my time," he recounted.

To complete its goal, Lester would need to win six consecutive playoff games. Just like in the NBA and college, the middle school playoffs were basically a whole new season. To capture the city ti-tle, they would need to win three games in three days, before mov-ing on to the state, held in a gym in another rough area, known as Whitehaven, just south of Memphis, where the Lions would have to win three more times over the course of four days if they were to walk away with the big trophy. Their first game in the city playoffs was against Hamilton, the third time the two teams had met. No coach wants to face a team for a third time in a season after beat-ing them the two previous games. Simple odds come against you.

Fortunately Reggie and Robert took over in the first half and Hamilton didn't have an answer. The boys scored at will, grabbed loose balls, and blocked shots. When Robert tipped the ball in just before the halftime buzzer, Lester held a commanding 36–17 edge.

The Lions maintained that advantage for much of the second half.

With 3:14 left in the game, Lester led 59–42. But after several quick steals, Hamilton cut the lead to 61–49 with just under two minutes. The tension could be felt among Lester fans. They were cussing and screaming—in disbelief that they were not finishing off Hamilton with ease. The Wildcats clamped down and forced several more quick turnovers, scoring off each one. The game was 61–55 with 1:04 remaining.

Clinging to the six-point lead, Reggie got fouled immediately.

He went to the free throw line and made both. On the ensuing play, a Hamilton guard darted up court for an easy layup. The score stood at Lester 63, Hamilton 57 with thirty-six seconds left. Hamilton's school slogan is:

If I believe, I can achieve
If I achieve, I will succeed
In meeting the challenges of the 21st century.

The Wildcats were meeting the challenge posed by Lester. Hamilton stole the inbounds pass and launched a three-pointer. *Swish!*

The lead was sliced to three, 63–60. All momentum had shifted to Hamilton. The Lions were withering in clutch time, and this time they were in danger of losing. If Lester choked, their season would be over, short of their goal. The ball was fed to Robert on the block. The star turned and tossed up a bank shot that rolled off the rim. After a mad scramble, the Wildcats emerged with the ball and called time-out.

With a three-pointer, Hamilton had a chance to tie the game at the buzzer. If that happened, Lester would likely fold, too distraught over what might've been. Hamilton's coach drew up the play.

After taking the inbounds pass, a Hamilton guard rose in the air to shoot a three. But the ball slipped from his hands, and Lester's Courtney McLemore snatched it away to seal a dramatic, albeit sloppy, 63–60 victory. Like any coach in the playoffs, Penny was happy to move on. He expected a blowout, but as the cliché goes, A win is a win. The Lions were still alive.

The next night on the same neutral court was equally nerveracking against Vance. Lester trailed 20–17 at halftime, one of the few times all season they were behind at half. The game remained tight throughout, with both teams trading the lead. Amid the hectic pace of the fourth quarter, Penny shed his dark gray blazer. He couldn't take control of the game like in his playing days. All he could hope for was that the players would carry through with his guidance. He remained calm, seated in his folding chair. He was the epitome of cool under pressure.

With twenty seconds remaining, Lester held a 43–40 advantage. Kobe passed the ball to Robert. Big men aren't known for being good free throw shooters, so Vance players immediately fouled him. Robert walked to the charity stripe. The opposing fans hissed. Robert glanced over at Penny. The former NBA all-star pumped his fist and gave an approving nod. Robert swished the first free throw, then nailed the second one. It was 45–40 with fifteen seconds left.

Vance turned the ball over on its next possession and fouled Robert again. He finished off Vance with two more free throws. Lester walked away with a 47–40 victory in the semifinals of the city tournament.

The only thing that stood between Lester and the Memphis city championship was the Memphis Academy of Health Sciences, best known as MAHS, one of the first charter schools in Tennessee history. The school is sponsored by 100 Black Men of Memphis, a group of city power players whose goal is "intellectual development of youth and the economic empowerment of the African-American community based upon the following precepts: respect for family, spirituality, justice, and integrity."

The school is working on building a strong tradition, both in academics and athletics. But MAHS had a major height disadvantage against Lester. Their tallest player was about 5-foot-11. Penny and Dez had a simple strategy: Feed the ball to Robert and Reggie and let them go to work.

The contest would take place at Colonial Middle School, a gym with a red, white, and blue theme throughout to match the patriot mascot. In the locker room, the boys of Lester sat on a bench. Penny discussed defenses. He praised Robert for hustling against Vance and intimidating their shooters by putting pressure on them along the baseline. "Reggie, you've just got to do the same thing," Penny said. "You've just got to recognize when some shooters are down there."

Reggie shook his head.

"Now, what are you shaking your head for?" Penny said.

Reggie: "Who me?"

"Yeah, I'm telling the truth," Penny said. "What do you want me to say? Come on. You've just got to come off your block. This is your team, man. They need you. You ain't got to put your head down every time I say something that's real.

"Come on, Reggie," Penny continued. "Get your head up. You're supposed to be a leader on this team. You know what I mean? If you're a leader, be a leader. It's simple: Ain't nobody more athletic than you in middle school, ain't nobody stronger than you, ain't nobody jumping like you. Save it for the game, and we'll get over on them on the floor."

Penny brought the boys in. "We're gonna say a prayer right now." They bowed their heads and said the Lord's Prayer.

It was game time.

Penny put on a navy blazer to match the rest of his suit. Dez looked dapper in a jet-black suit—the Johnny Cash of basketball. The two walked onto the court after the team pranced out. The Lester Lions carried an impressive 19-3 record.

"It's the battle of the *city*!" the announcer said.

MAHS seemed overwhelmed from the start. Robert won the tip-off and within the first five seconds got an offensive rebound and bucket. Reggie immediately stole the ball. Nick, Courtney, and Demarcus passed the ball around on the perimeter.

"Robert overload! Overload!" Penny yelled.

Robert moved down low to the other block. Courtney passed it to him. With three guys hanging on to him, Robert turned and swished it. The Lions were off and running. Reggie scored next to make it 6–0.

Robert Washington showing off his own thundering dunk.

MAHS didn't have an answer.

On the next possession, Robert got three offensive rebounds in a single trip. The MAHS players were scratching and clawing at him—anything to stop his dominance. "Atta way to hang in there, Robert," Dez said.

Robert nailed two free throws. It was 8–0 in the first minute of play. The lead swelled to 14–0 before MAHS made a shot. Lester didn't let up. Nick hit two three-pointers from the same exact spot on the left wing.

"For *threeeeeeee*! Nick Merriweather!" the announcer shouted.

Lester was up 20–2 at the end of the first quarter.

The teams played a slow tempo in the second quarter with each struggling to score. Lester took a 28–9 lead into halftime. Robert had a monster half: 15 points, 10 rebounds, and 3 blocks.

Penny reminded the team in the locker room what happened two days earlier against Hamilton. "Let's learn from Hamilton Middle, because everything's not easy for us," he said. "Let's jump on them and go hard in the third quarter. If we jump on them and go hard, they're gonna give up. They already want to give up. But if you let them back in the game, that referee is gonna turn on their side."

The MAHS Lions came out prepared. They weren't ready to throw in the towel. MAHS outscored Lester 9 to 5 in the first three minutes of the second half. Then, with 2:17 left in the quarter, one of its guards stole the ball and cut to the basket to trim Lester's advantage to 33–20. The MAHS fans finally had something to cheer about; they rose to their feet, chanting in unison, "Defense! Defense!"

For a brief moment, it seemed Lester might let up, as they had done so many times before in the second half. But Robert took over, showing his true star potential. The next trip up court, he fired a three from the right baseline to silence the MAHS contingent: 36–20. He finished the quarter with four more points, to extend the lead to 40–22.

It was the death knell for MAHS. They never recovered. Robert finished his MVP performance with 31 points, 19 rebounds, and 7 blocks. Lester walked away with a 58–27 victory and the city championship.

One goal down. But Penny and Dez wanted to make history. Their sights were set on the state.

CHAPTER 14

From Death to Life

Rev. Larry Peoples scanned the crowd in the bleachers at Lester. It was impossible to look at the faces of the gang members and not reflect on the mistakes of his own life. He prayed not for team wins, but for victories off the court.

Long before Larry became a prayer warrior for the Lester Lions basketball team. Long before Larry stood in Desmond's hospital room praying over him. Before all of that, Larry ruled Binghampton decked out in his pimped-out trench coat, major jewelry, and alligator shoes. His favorite ring was decorated with an oil well, marked by a two-carat diamond. Money flowed through his hands as freely as oil in Texas. He even had a Rolls-Royce.

"You need a grocery cart to carry his rap sheet into the courtroom," said Antoine Richardson, Reggie Green's grandfather. "Oh, my man, Larry Peoples! He was one of the baddest dudes around. He walked around with a pistol all the time. He was gonna get him some money. When you seen him coming, you'd better cover your jewelry. It'd be Friday, and you'd be tucking in your gold because here he comes. He had more jewelry than Mr. T."

Antoine was no patron saint himself. He served several years in prison for drug dealing. Once, when he was released, he attended

Antoine Richardson with the Rev. Larry Peoples.

Zion Temple church in Binghampton because "I was changing my life around." He closed his eyes and prayed one day, then felt a strong hand on his head. "Next thing I know, Larry Peoples come outta nowhere and grabs me. He's saying, 'Please, Lord, rebuke Satan. Get it out of him!' I opened my eyes, looked up, and said, 'Oh, Lord, it's Larry Peoples. I ain't getting out of this headlock.'"

He would've been terrified in prior years, but he had heard in prison that Larry had changed. He never quite believed it, at least not until that moment.

"His pistol now is his Bible," Antoine said.

I heard similar stories of Larry for weeks, the notorious gangster turned evangelist. I heard the tales so often I began to wonder if he was urban legend, that Larry Peoples was a metaphor and didn't really exist. Then one day I opened the door at Dez's apartment. The 6-foot-2 Larry was dressed in Penny's OneCent gear. And like in Antoine's story, before I knew it, my head was bowed and Larry placed his hand on my head. I swear I felt a jolt from my head to my toes. I had to contain myself from hollering, *Hallelujah!* I wanted to tell him to take me straight to the Mississippi River, dunk my white butt in the murky waters, and cleanse my soul.

Instead I hopped in his car for what can best be described as a rolling revival in the River City. Larry drove. His young son was late to an event, and so I took a seat in the back. He spoke of the Prodigal Son, who strayed only to come back home. He talked about how he faced more than twenty life sentences—but got paroled and returned to Binghampton. He spoke of the blight of the community, what was destroying black families in the inner city.

"Life is about choices, and the devil is always trying to get you to make the wrong choice," he screeched. "Everything's glitter and gold. It looks good to your eyes, but it's not good for your soul.

"This generation, they're caught up gangbanging. You've got parents, which are children, having children. How's a child supposed to teach a child life lessons? A child can't teach a child nothing. The TV is doing all the teaching.

"God didn't create a child to be birthed in this world without the father and mother, because it takes both of them to raise a child. A father has a responsibility, just like a mother has a responsibility. When you turn around and separate either one of them, it makes it very difficult on the child. You know what I'm saying?"

He looked in his rearview mirror to catch my eyes, to make sure I was listening. His son sat in the passenger seat, mostly oblivious to our conversation. Larry's voice was smooth, punctuated by his warm smile. He can speak of the ills of Binghampton, because he personified it. He was raised by his grandma. Never had a relationship with his dad. His mom was around, but his stepdad rejected him. "My grandmother provided me with everything I needed, yet she was gone working long hours and working jobs as a maid. That left time where I was alone."

His first crime was stealing little stuff as a kid. He saw some toy cowboys and Indians on a corner rack in a local grocery store. "Following the wicked spirit of the devil, I was stealing something that didn't belong to me. Stole it and got away with it. But the next time, I tried it again and got caught." He went back home and hid out in the bathroom. His grandmother happened to go to the store to pay her grocery bill when she was told of Larry's errors. She stormed into the bathroom, where he was in the tub. "She got to hollering: 'I'm not raising you to take things that don't belong to you, and you're up there stealing.'" She pulled out a belt and snapped it in the air. "She whipped my tail real good. Then she made me get dressed, without a shirt, and told me to take that stuff back to the owner.

"Seems like that beating, that whupping, that discipline would've changed me. But as I got older, I started mingling with other kids doing stuff I had no business doing. I got caught up in the lane they call pimping. Got caught up in there having all these different types of women doing things for me."

He had been a star basketball player in the late 1960s, taking off from just beneath the free throw line to dunk. "That's when dunking was illegal. You'd get a technical," he said. Colleges began recruiting him in the ninth grade, he said, but he had already determined "women was the way, instead of going through college and getting my degree.

"God was opening up doors for me, but I was too stupid and ignorant to even see. I had demons in me that I allowed to live."

His car zipped between traffic on the highway.

The revival rolled on.

As Larry explained it, he did go off to college to play ball for Lane College, the same black college in Jackson, Tennessee, that Desmond attended. He had no intentions of ever graduating. "I couldn't get in my books because I was too busy stealing, pimping, burglarizing. All kinds of things. I wasn't upholding my scholarship and so I dropped out. And when I dropped out, I started doing everything."

Pimping, dealing cocaine and marijuana, gambling, loansharking. You name it, Larry had his hands in it. "I was not knowing the devil was trying to take my life.

"The Lord's bringing it all back to me today," he said with a smile. He pressed the accelerator.

Back then, he kept women spread across Binghampton and the mid-South, to make it impossible for police to know exactly where he lived at any given moment. His cars were usually filled with guns, CB radios, tape players—loot he'd stolen around town. When you're dealing with the devil's work, he said, you make enemies. In 1975 he had threatened to kill a john who owed him thousands of dollars. "I was coming to collect it, and the police busted me." He was convicted of extortion, two counts of crime against nature, and committing a felony with a firearm.

At the age of twenty-two, he faced fifteen years in prison. He was paroled in 1983.

"You'd have thought I would've learned my lesson. I said I was done dealing with women, that I'd only stick with one. I started off like I was, but the love of money is the root of all evil. There's nothing wrong with money, but when you worship it as your God, it'll overtake you."

The car whizzed through a suburban landscape, with its Longhorn Steakhouse, Olive Garden, a Toys 'R' Us. "I was trying to do my best when I got out of prison, but what was in me came back out."

He started robbing all the time. Hotel robberies became easy pickings. It also became his undoing. He robbed five people at gunpoint at a Memphis hotel, but got captured soon afterward. He faced twenty-one armed robbery charges, four counts of assault with intent to rob, and one count for receiving stolen property. Each of the armed robbery charges carried a maximum life sentence. He decided to plead guilty in 1987, figuring it was his best chance to ever see the free world again. He was sentenced to forty-five years.

"I'm the only man with more than twenty life sentences to be walking free today," he said. His car sat at a stoplight. "Praise Jesus. This is my testimony!"

Most of his time was spent in the Tennessee state penitentiary in Nashville. But he also served time in another prison, the Cold Creek Correctional Facility, also called Fort Pillow, in Henning, Tennessee, outside Memphis.

Inside prison, he maintained his grip. He said he controlled marijuana distribution, loansharked, gambled. He fixed dice so that he would win.

"But in 1990, this is when my life changed," he said.

Animosity had built between Larry and another inmate, nicknamed Country Earl. (I couldn't help but think a good southern tale isn't complete without a bad guy named Country Earl.)

As Larry recalled, Country Earl concocted a plot to steal ten thousand dollars' worth of Larry's jewelry. Larry always used his jewelry to sucker others in. Whether it was shooting dice or poker, inmates salivated, sure they'd win his jewels. But Country Earl had a new plan: He'd "get my jewelry and get me locked up on Death Row." Those involved believed Larry would kill his roommate when the jewelry turned up missing. He kept his jewels in his socks. It was a masterful two-for-one plan: They'd get Larry's jewelry and get rid of him.

"But God had other plans," he said. "I went to that sock, my heart dropped because it was light as a feather. I got on my cell mate and squeezed him. He's crying and carrying on. I'm up all night fuming. Man, I was crazy. Like a demon possessed."

His car slowed and pulled into a driveway. Out stepped his son for the party.

"I was going to kill everybody involved," he said as he backed the car up. "That was my plan, and I was going to make them wonder in advance how they'd die.

"But God cut all that stuff off." His voice rose to a crescendo. Tears streamed down his face as he lifted both hands from the steering wheel. His body trembled. The car zoomed down the interstate.

He said he called his grandmother that day, before the killing spree was to hatch.

"This is gonna blow your mind," he said. "I called home this particular day and my grandmother was speaking in tongues. I was used to that. But when she got done speaking in tongues, she started speaking in English and she told me what God had told her. I wouldn't dare tell my grandma that I was fixing to kill six people. All of a sudden, she said, 'GOD TOLD ME WHAT THE DEVIL'S FIXING TO MAKE YOU DO. IF YOU LET THE DEVIL MAKE A FOOL OUT OF YOU, I MIGHT AS WELL TELL THE LORD TO TAKE ME AND SEND ME ON TO GLORY. GOD ALREADY TOLD ME HE'S GOING TO SAVE YOU, HE'S GOING TO SANCTIFY YOU, HE'S GOING TO DELIVER YOU AND BRING YOU HOME.'"

The car flew down the highway. Larry squinted so hard that I couldn't tell if his eyes were open or shut. I considered leaping across and grabbing the steering wheel. "When I hung up that telephone, I was still gonna do it. Six men were gonna die."

He said he began to head to his cell. The annex had two floors and was made like a V, with officers stationed at that point. Larry walked the route toward his cell as he'd done countless times. It was 1990, Penny Hardaway's senior season in high school. A voice echoed across the prison block: *"This is your last chance."*

"I thought it was somebody messing with me," he said. "I heard this voice. I looked down the hall and didn't see nobody. I backed up and shut the door and didn't see no one."

His entire body trembled. Tears flowed. I wondered if God was driving the car, because it was beyond me how we had not crashed into a ditch. "Hallelujah! Thank you, Jesus," he screamed.

"I turned around and looked at the officer's station. Didn't see nobody," he said. "When He spoke, I didn't know God. So I'm looking for a man in the flesh and blood. And He said it again: *This is your last chance.*"

His voice cracked and wailed. "When I heard that second voice, I knew it was God speaking to me. I went to my room, A-138, and I fell on my knees and prayed at the foot of the bed. I was so deep in sin. And that day, I made a vow to serve the Lord to my very last day, and I've been serving Him ever since 1990."

His prayers were answered shortly before Christmas 1997. Larry Peoples, the man sentenced to forty-five years in 1987, was paroled. He walked out of prison at 9 A.M. on December 22, 1997.

"I'm gonna leave here for good," he told fellow inmates.

His car rolled to a stop at Desmond's place. My revival had come to an end. "I was lucky enough to have an old praying grandmother who never gave up on me," he said.

Larry Peoples. Thug. Criminal. Pimp. Coke dealer. He cherished a much different title now: reverend. He can be found on any given Sunday at Zion Temple in Binghampton. Stop in and see him, but be prepared. His pistol is his Bible, as Antoine said.

Larry's tale seemed so far-fetched, so outrageous that I believed he might be the best southern storyteller of all time, a classic yarn spinner who embellished most everything. *Like really, who gets freed from prison ten years into a forty-five-year sentence?*

I contacted the Tennessee Department of Correction. His rap sheet indeed stretched for more than two pages, including twenty-one counts of robbery with a deadly weapon in 1987. He had pleaded guilty and was sentenced to forty-five years.

"Wow, he was busy," said Dorinda Carter, a spokeswoman for the agency, as she scrolled through the list of charges.

She said Larry had thirty-four total convictions dating back to 1976, including an extortion charge from a 1975 offense. He was disciplined four times in prison in the early 1980s for "possession of free world money, drug possession, selling drugs, and possession of contraband." She noted that during the time he was in prison, it was much easier for gangsters to maintain their control of drug distribution, even while locked up.

Larry now has to check in monthly with a parole officer, until the year 2025. At his most recent meeting, she said, "it stated that Mr. Peoples continues to be gainfully employed, has no new arrests, and Mr. Peoples states he has no complaints or concerns at this time." She confirmed he was paroled just before Christmas 1997.

Before I left him that day, he told me one more thing. "From death to life, that's Desmond's story. That's Binghampton's story."

CHAPTER 15

Chemo Drip

Coach Dez limped across the gray linoleum floor of the waiting room at St. Francis Hospital in East Memphis. He hated the place, its dull peach walls and 1970s office furniture matching the gloomy moods of so many of the cancer patients in the room. He strolled down a hall and past the sign that served as a reminder of how sick he was: "Children 12 and under are not allowed in the Chemotherapy Room." He walked through the door. There were fifteen beige recliners made of fake leather—five on each wall—to match the beige paint and beige floor.

"Attention, please do not place any food wrappers, cups, cans, or newspapers in red bucket," read the pink laminated paper sign. The red bucket was for biohazards only.

A nurse hooked up three IVs to Dez's right shoulder, where he had an implant to readily flow chemo. The drip of toxic chemicals began the start of a four-hour process. He had never told the team he was still sick. But twice a month, on Mondays, he made the wretched trek.

The chemo worked its way into his body. An oxygen machine of a nearby patient wheezed every few seconds.

It had been a year since his lifesaving surgery, when Penny visited him in his room, when Rev. Larry Peoples prayed for his soul. He thought of the promise he'd made long ago: to be the best father he could be, to return to Binghampton to mentor the kids of Lester, to coach them to a state championship. The positive mentors in his life flashed through his mind: his grandfather, the Memphis Duck, Antoine Richardson, Walter Casey of the Lester Community Center, his high school coach Reginald Mosby. His thoughts focused most on Coach Mosby. It was he who inspired Dez to return to basketball as a coach. "He prepared me for the situation with cancer, just to be strong. If it weren't for him, I don't think I would've survived. I probably would've given up," Dez said. "He would never let me give up on anything. . . . He was like my dad. He was there when I needed him the most, as far as just being a young man and coming up out of this neighborhood. We could've easily have gone out here and gotten into crime and started all kinds of stupid stuff. But he made sure we stayed on the right path."

Some days in the chemo room, a country boy sat across from Dez wearing a baseball cap with the Confederate flag. Dez was too busy to notice on this day. He had bigger things on his mind.

It was the start of Championship Week. The Lester Lions rolled in the city championship against MAHS, powered by Robert Washington's 31 points, 19 rebounds, and 7 blocks. To win the state, the Lions would need to win three straight games. They had made it this far the previous year, only to lose to Union City in the semifinals. To win it all, he believed he would need his four veteran players to step up: Reggie, Kobe the Mayor, Courtney McLemore, and his son, Nick. Dez was feeling the least confident about Robert. He had had a spectacular season, averaging 23 points and 17 rebounds a game, but his mental toughness was questionable. He had walked out on the team eight times during the season. How could he be counted on in the state when the game was on the line?

Dez placed a white blanket over his head, closed his eyes, and drifted off to sleep.

CHAPTER 16

Don't Quit

The team's star ran out of the gym, down Johnson Avenue, across Tillman Street, and hid inside his grandmother's asbestos-shingled home. Robert ran like he was being chased and, in fact, Penny was in pursuit. Penny had seen too many championships escape. He wasn't going to let that happen. The former NBA all-star jumped in his Cadillac Escalade and sped to Robert's home.

He texted Robert's mom, then his aunt. He called, too.

Lester's chances of winning the state without Robert were slim. Penny told his aunt to get Robert outside of the house. Now! But even more than that, the long-term ramifications if Robert didn't suit up would prove too costly. High schools would blackball him, leaving another Memphis ballplayer to potentially fall to the streets. He would ruin a rare chance to prove his worth on the big stage.

As was typical, the news spread through Binghampton and, within minutes, more than fifty people stood outside. They were texting and calling everyone.

Robert refused to come out. He used his younger brothers and sisters to relay a message to Penny: "Basketball's not for me. I don't want to play no more."

Auntie Shree talked with him. Like he'd done throughout the season, Robert pretended as if he didn't have practice. She recalled the conversation as starting off calm, before she grew tired of his lies.

"Robert, please don't do this," she said she told him. "You have everybody in Binghampton saying good things about you and your play. Don't let these people down. Prove something to your father: Let him know what he's missing out on. But right now you've got little boys up at that gym saying Robert's a quitter. Are you going to be a quitter all your life?"

And when that didn't work, Shree said she went in for the slam dunk.

"YOU WILL NOT QUIT THIS TEAM! GET YOUR BUTT UP THERE TO YOUR TEAM AND DO WHAT YOU NEED TO DO, BECAUSE WE'RE GOING TO WIN THIS CHAMPIONSHIP!"

He slinked out and got in Penny's Caddy. "Sorry, Penny," he said repentantly.

CHAPTER 17

Going Places

The players for Airways Middle School, a Memphis city school located on Ketchum Road near Memphis International Airport, practiced layup drills. The Jets had reached the finals two years earlier, only to lose. Two players from that team went on to star at powerhouse Melrose High School, which had produced All-American William Bedford in the 1980s. Dressed in red jerseys with blue trim, the Airways players had deep looks of intensity—wide eyes and expressionless faces—as they warmed up. The Jets were a good team but lacked depth. They were 20-point under-dogs against the Lions, who everyone in the gym pegged to breeze through the state playoffs.

Led by Reggie Green and Kobe "the Mayor" Freeman, the Lester Lions burst out of the locker room, circled the Airways' end of the court to intimidate them, and met at center court giving low fives. They then sprinted toward the basket on their end in a quick succession of layup drills. They seemed so perfectly choreographed they could've been an opening act for Cirque du Soleil.

The Lester players were decked out in long-sleeve warm-up tops with a Lion emblazoned on the front. To further pump up the team, a boom box rattled off the Lions' rap song:

Super fly swag
You can say my flag's flying
Yeah, I'm a Lion

Penny walked onto the court in a tailored brown suit. Dez matched, but without the blazer. The court this night was at Geeter Middle School in Whitehaven, about twenty minutes from Binghampton. It was host to the tournament, from February 4 to February 10. The fans from Lester filled one entire side of the gym. The Airways' section was nearly empty. The crowd drew silent as starters were announced: Nick Merriweather, Courtney McLemore, Demarcus Martin, Robert Washington.

"Last but not least," the announcer crooned, "Reggiiiiiiiiiieeeeeeeee Green." Reggie ran onto the court and high-fived Kobe before joining the rest of the starters near center court.

Players for both teams were nervous, and it showed immediately after tip-off. Both teams had quick turnovers. Penny had told the team beforehand to take it easy, that this was the first step in getting to where they wanted. The Jets' first shot was blocked by Robert Washington.

Nick Merriweather racing in for a layup.

Airways packed in its defense, playing a tight zone to contain Robert and Reggie. Their plan was to force the 6-4 Robert to play on the perimeter rather than down low by the basket. The strategy worked early on. Lester couldn't play its run-and-gun style. Airways made the Lions slow the pace down, taking twenty to thirty seconds off the clock on each possession. Both teams struggled with shots—even ones from two feet away, a sign of rattled nerves on the big stage.

But Demarcus finally found Reggie on the block to break through the ice for a 2–0 lead. Soon Demarcus had his first bucket, after a nice feed from Courtney off an offensive rebound. But an Airways guard countered immediately with a three-pointer to make it 4–3.

The Lions decided to ride their money man. Reggie got it in the paint and was hammered on a shot. As he concentrated on his free throw, the Jets cheerleaders chanted: "Miss it! Come on, miss it!" He clanked the first off the front of the rim, but he made the second. It was only 5–3 nearly halfway through the first quarter. Neither team seemed to be able to do anything. Players were unwilling to step up, or too nervous to do so. Perhaps a combination of both.

After several sloppy trips up court by both teams, Courtney twice broke free, adding two consecutive baskets to stretch the lead to 9–3. Nick stole the ball on Airways' next possession and found Robert from beyond the arc. The big man stood just to the right of the top of the key and let it fly.

Bingo!

Down 12–3 with less than a minute remaining in the first quarter, the Jets were crashing and burning. If they had a mayday button, they would've pressed it. When they missed another easy shot from five feet out, Reggie ripped off the rebound and passed it to Nick, who darted up court. Robert lingered on the left baseline from twenty-two feet out. Nick hit him with the pass. Robert was in the zone. He stroked his second straight three-pointer, to end the quarter.

Lester was dominating, as the Lions always seemed to do in opening quarters. The score stood at 15–3 at the end of one. Airways could do nothing right. They struggled to get shots off. The sudden enthusiastic play of Lester's players was testament to how bad they wanted to win, for Coach Dez and themselves.

The opening minutes of the second quarter played out much the same. Lester's defense harassed Airways into several more turnovers. The Lions entered into a stall mode to take precious time off the clock. They were in no hurry to score, since the lead was so large.

Midway through the second quarter, Kobe cut to the basket and dished to Reggie for an easy layup. "Reggie GREEEEEEEEEN for two," the announcer screamed over the PA system.

It was 18–5.

But games change in a flash. It was as if Lester blinked and Airways was jet-propelled. An Airways guard sped up the floor coast to coast, hitting an acrobatic layup and getting fouled by Reggie in the process. With the free throw made, Airways sliced the lead to 18–8, giving Jets fans a glimmer of hope. It didn't seem like much at the time. It's not like Airways was gonna come back.

The teams battled for several more possessions. When Airways hit a layup to make it 19–10, Penny took off his blazer and paced the sidelines. He sensed something was amiss with his team. He knew that momentum swings like a pendulum. It didn't help matters that Lester suddenly went cold and Airways couldn't miss. They scored on three straight trips, to trim the Lion lead to 20–16. "Let's go Airways! Let's go!" the Jets fans chanted, suddenly with a burst of energy.

Lester continued to take time off the clock. They held the ball for twenty seconds before Nick fired a three-pointer that missed long and sent an Airways guard streaking up the court. It looked like he would lay it in to cut the lead to two but then Robert came out of nowhere to swat the ball out of bounds.

"Robert Washington with the block!" the announcer said.

The Jets quickly threw the ball back in and scored immediately to make it 20–18. "Number twenty-five for the Jets," the announcer said. The Airways fans rose to their feet, stomping and clapping. *"Defense! Defense!"*

The Jets defense tightened up and prevented Lester from scoring. As the buzzer sounded, the mighty Lions were on the ropes. They'd been kept to a single point—a penny—the final three minutes of the second quarter. Reggie finished the half with 7 points, 7 rebounds, and 2 steals. Robert had 6 points, on two-of-six shooting—all of them three-point attempts.

In the locker room, Penny told the team to push the pace, that the guards needed to settle down. He asked Robert why a 6-4 giant was setting up beyond the three-point line every trip up court, rather than posting up. He noted Robert didn't even attempt a shot from inside the three-point line. The Lions were playing straight into Airways' hands. That was the Jets' game plan. Don't fall for that, Penny said.

Lester responded in the opening minutes of the third quarter with a lockdown defense that forced several turnovers. Lester clung to a four-point advantage when Demarcus nailed a three-pointer from the left baseline: 27–20. The momentum swung back in favor of Lester.

Airways called time-out. Penny walked onto the court and gave Demarcus an *attaboy* high-five.

Both teams went back and forth for several trips. The third quarter ended with Lester up 29–24. The fourth quarter began with Robert stealing the ball, streaking toward the basket, cradling it, and laying it in for an amazing two points.

Lester seemingly had regained control of the ball game 31–24.

With less than five minutes to go, Penny paced the sidelines. He patted his head to indicate a slow-it-down pace. "Hold the ball," he shouted.

Following Penny's orders, Lester ticked off twelve seconds, then Robert got the ball underneath the basket. He couldn't resist going for another bucket, but his shot rimmed out. Penny motioned his players to intensify their defensive pressure. Usually calm and in his seat, Penny hadn't sat the whole fourth quarter. He wanted the win. Dez kept in his seat, barking out for the Lions to play sticky defense.

But just like that, Airways big man lowered his shoulder in the lane for an uncontested layup: Lester 31, Airways 26. The Lions quickly countered on two straight possessions to stretch it to 35–26 with just over three minutes. The Lions had finally delivered the knockout blow. Or so it seemed.

A game is never over until that final buzzer, especially at the middle school level, when players crack and others catch fire. With 2:30 left, Airways pushed the ball up court, trailing 35–28. One of its guards camped out in the corner from about twenty-two feet. *Swish!*

"THREEEEEEEE-pointer," the announcer said.

Holding a 35–31 lead, Lester took the clock under two minutes but failed to score on its next trip. An Airways guard pushed the tempo and passed to their main scorer, who got a great look from five feet away. The ball rolled around on the rim, then popped out. The Airways contingent let out a collective *"Ohhhhhh!"* Reggie snagged the rebound and called time-out.

"Bring it in," Dez said.

Penny told the players not to panic, that they were too talented to lose. On the inbounds, Reggie was mobbed at half-court and the ball squirmed free. Airways' star player picked up the loose ball on the left baseline, raced toward the goal, and scooped it up and under for a reverse layup with just over a minute. The score stood at 35–33.

The final minute was a hectic blur, but Lester escaped the upset with a couple of layups to move on. When the buzzer sounded, Lester was the victor of the quarterfinal with a 41–33 win.

Reggie finished with 15 points, 10 rebounds, 3 steals, and 1 block. Robert followed Penny's instruction. He didn't shoot a single three-pointer in the second half. He wound up with 14 points, 7 rebounds, and 5 blocks.

It wasn't pretty, but it was a victory and edged them closer to their goal—two victories away from winning the state.

The Lara Kendall Falcons took to the court in their green and gold uniforms, riding a seven-game winning streak. Their record stood at 16-4. The school, located a hundred miles north of Memphis, near the Kentucky border, is tiny, with about two hundred kids in middle school grades. The team from Lake County, one of the poorest rural counties in America, had beaten Lester in the playoffs two years earlier, in Dez's first season. Dez had revenge on his mind, as did Reggie Green.

The Falcons were powered by a pure shooter named Darius Johnson, who averaged 21 points a game. He had a deft touch from the three-point line, but could also get physical when called upon. The Falcons' other top player had suffered a season-ending injury. The Falcons' coach, David Ayers, knew his team would have to play the perfect game to win. They didn't have a single player over 6 feet. Ayers had two guys, both 5-9, to guard Reggie and Robert. He told his team that if they didn't box out, Lester would dominate.

It was an intimidating thought. It got even more so when Coach Ayers looked at who was manning the sidelines as Lester's coach. He had seen Penny Hardaway in the stands a few nights earlier. He believed Penny was there just to watch basketball. Some of his players had even introduced themselves and asked for Penny's autograph.

He realized, though, that Penny was his nemesis this day. "I was like 'Oh my goodness.'"

When Lester took the court, the music blared; the bass thumped. The gym began rocking to the Lions' theme song. The Binghampton contingent grew louder and louder. Coach Ayers spied the Lester side of the court. He couldn't believe the size of Lester's two big men. He also noticed their uniforms. Their warm-ups were nicer than those of most Division I schools, arguably better than some NBA franchises'. "Dang," Coach Ayers said. "Penny hooked them up."

At 6-7, Coach Ayers met eye to eye with Penny. The two shook hands. Penny was cordial, even nice.

But with his team, Penny was all business. He told the boys of Lester that they had come too far to lose. All the work they put in on a daily basis—the extra laps, the academic work, everything—had come down to this. Would they walk away short of their goal or put themselves in a position to win it all—to make their families and Binghampton proud? Penny asked.

Dez reinforced that point. He said it was time to take care of business. Losing was not an option.

The Falcons quieted the boisterous Binghampton crowd shortly after tip-off. They jumped out to a 6–2 lead and appeared to have control in the early part of the first quarter. Lester had the jitters. Their guards turned the ball over. But the Lions caught a huge break when Falcons star Darius Johnson got whistled for his second foul in just the first three minutes. He was yanked from the game.

With the Falcons' best player on the sidelines, the Lions went to work. Their defense intensified. They played a 1-3-1 defense, with Reggie on top. It confused the Falcons' guards. They couldn't make a shot. On the offensive end, Reggie and Robert couldn't be stopped. They just kept coming and coming. Lester kept the Falcons scoreless for the remainder of the quarter, ending with an 11–6 advantage. Penny told them not to let up, that they needed to keep the Run going while Darius was on the bench. And they responded. They went for the jugular like a lion jumping on a weakened elephant.

The Lions came in waves off the bench. They were too fast, too big, too deep. Then Reggie broke free. He took off from about three feet in front of the free throw line. He cocked his arm back, his elbow above the rim, and threw the ball down so hard it seemed the backboard might break. The goal shook from side to side. The Lester fans erupted with jubilant celebration. "Oooooooooooo!" Antoine Richardson shouted. "Boy's been working on his game! Ain't never seen him throw down like that." Penny pumped his fist. Dez did, too.

Even Coach Ayers was impressed. "That dunk was something you'd see in the NBA. Their fans were going nuts. I don't know who wouldn't have. It was unbelievable."

On the Falcons sideline Darius jumped from the bench and ran to the scorer's table to check in. He wasn't meant to be watching from the sidelines. He needed to be on the court if his team had any shot at coming back. Coach Ayers called a time-out. He wasn't a quitter, nor was his team. But he knew the game was over. The damage was done.

There was no way Lester was going to lose.

The Lions held a 26–10 lead at halftime. They kept Darius to just 4 points in limited playing time. Meanwhile, they produced an

all-around team effort. In the second quarter, Alex Lomax scored
5 points; Reggie and Robert chipped in 3 points apiece; Courtney
had a bucket, as did Albert Zleh.

It was one of the most solid all-around quarters of the entire
season.

Penny gathered his troops at half. The team had seen too many
leads disappear. He told them to stay composed, to play their
game until the final buzzer sounded. They placed their hands together and shouted their fight motto: "All for one, one for all, all
for Lester!"

The Falcons didn't relent. They made a charge in the third
quarter. But as soon as it seemed momentum had shifted, the ball
came to Nick Merriweather, who drained a three-pointer. "It just
killed my kids," Coach Ayers said. "He was a little engine. He just
kept running and running and running. He was fun to watch."

The Falcons hung tough, but the early Lester lead was too
much. The Lions built up confidence early and weren't going to let
up in this game. The third quarter ended with Lester ahead by 17
points, the score 40–23.

Reggie and Robert got rebound after rebound. It was as if the
two teen sensations were guarded by dwarves. They were impossible to stop. "Those two kids were something else," recalled Coach
Ayers.

When the buzzer sounded, the final score was Lester 54, Lara
Kendall 34. Reggie finished with 15 points and 15 rebounds; Robert ended with a solid game: 12 points and 11 boards.

Coach Ayers was impressed with how well coached—and well
disciplined—the team was. "I tell everybody, 'Hey, look, I lost to
Penny Hardaway's team.'"

The Lester Lions stood one win away from capturing their goal.

CHAPTER 18

The Enforcers

Memphis native Chris Garner doesn't need to be reminded of the violence that plagues his hometown. He sees it every day on the faces of boys ranging in age from eleven to seventeen—adolescents who never had fathers, never had anyone care for them, never had mentors. Many put gang life above everything and have no deference for authority or adults.

He tries to rehabilitate the troubled boys as part of a second-chance program to turn their lives around.

For Chris, it's also personal. He lived a couple of houses down when Penny got shot in college. That moment was a reminder that "your life can be taken in a flash." A 5-9 point guard, Chris followed Penny's footsteps at Treadwell High in the early 1990s and then at the University of Memphis. For two years in college, he roomed with Lorenzen Wright, whose murder in a wooded area in suburban Memphis in July 2010 remains unsolved. "Every day I wake up, it goes through my mind," he said. He doesn't believe reports that Lorenzen was caught up in the lane dealing drugs. "Lorenzen wasn't that type of guy, from the time I knew him to the time that they found him.

"He made enough money where he didn't have to do those

types of activities," he said. "But in today's times, we have to be careful. We have to watch where we go, watch who we hang with."

Basketball allowed Chris to see the world. He played brief stints in the NBA and eleven years overseas in Lithuania, France, Greece, Cyprus, and Israel, making a couple of million dollars along the way. He invested his money wisely. And like Penny, he has returned to his roots.

His court now is altogether different. He teaches at-risk boys in a program called Youth Dimensions, based in a forty-eight-bed lockdown facility for boys who are in the custody of the Tennessee Department of Children's Services. Its mission is to foster an "environment that encourages personal, cultural, and educational growth to the children and adolescents we serve."

"I can relate to the kids because I know some of them have just been dealt a bad hand," Chris said. "I tell them: Just because you made a mistake now doesn't mean your life is over. I get up every day with the mind-set of trying to get just one of these kids to know that it's not over—that just because you failed today, tomorrow is still a promising day.

"If you can help just four, five, six, or seven out of fifty, you feel good."

He said he was mentored by the best—that Penny took him under his wing years ago and that he feels compelled to help because of that. "It wasn't so much the things he taught me on the court. It was more the things off the court," Chris told me as he hung out with friends in Binghampton. "He always sat down with me and talked with me about being humble, about being respectable, about presenting yourself in a professional manner. At that particular time, you had to present yourself in a way that people would accept you. He helped me a lot on the journey I went on."

Success comes with incremental steps at the Youth Dimensions facility. He celebrates with his students when they pass the GED. Many of the boys resist change, their allegiances already ingrained in them. "I'm just trying to teach these kids that there's more to life than gangbanging and colors and finger signs," he said. "It's not about the streets. It's about growing up, trying to raise a family, and trying to be a role model for your family when you do have kids."

He uses his status as a retired professional ballplayer to break through. "No matter what happens, no matter where you live, if you want it bad enough and you put in the work, then it can happen. I'm a living witness to that."

He knows all too well the cautionary tale of what happens to boys with no intervention. Even for those with mentors, the forces working against them in a violent city like Memphis are like a black hole—always tugging on the area kids, even when they resist. Today's gang members have elevated social status among teens, he said. They don't respect the unwritten rules of the previous generation—when Memphis gangs backed off ballplayers and supported them because they possessed a future beyond crime.

"I absolutely believe the streets are more dangerous today," he said. "They're not afraid of anything."

Violence may be what grabs the headlines: *If it bleeds, it leads*. But there's a determined force of powerful black men trying to turn the tide in Memphis, a new generation with the power and money to make a difference. Many were schooled under Larry Finch, the late University of Memphis basketball coach who taught them to never forget their roots, that they were to return to mentor kids when their careers ended. They want to shed the image of Memphis basketball players as thugs.

"That's a part of what I call the city of Memphis, the city of good abode. That's almost to be expected," said U.S. Attorney Ed Stanton, the prosecutor leading the gang crackdown.

Across Memphis, you can find the old gym rats, their hair a bit gray, barking out signals on the sidelines. Keith Lee, the 6-10 All-American power forward who dominated the collegiate ranks during the 1980s, coaches high school ball.

Andre Turner, the Little General whose buzzer beaters propelled Memphis State to the Final Four in 1985, returned to his alma mater, Mitchell High School, to be an assistant. Andre played four years in the NBA, shuttling between seven teams. He played another fourteen years professionally overseas, in Spain, finally retiring at the age of forty-four. Like other former Tiger stars, he came back home to pass on his life lessons to the new vulnerable generation. He helps coach in the gym bearing his name.

"I wanted to see them be good basketball players, but the most important part of our little journey was watching them become better young men. That will get them further in life," Andre said. "That was part of my first speech. Being honorable, being somebody of your word and owning up to it was what was most important to me. From the start of the season to the end, you could see the guys grow."

He never asked the players if they were involved with gangs. "All I was concerned about was them being responsible young men. When they showed up, they were under our jurisdiction. We told them we're not going to let you do things you're not supposed to do," Andre said. "We would see growth, almost each day. That was the greatest feeling about it."

They scheduled shooting drills for 6 A.M., before school, followed by a couple of hours of practice after the final bell—to keep the Mitchell players in the gym for as long as possible and off the streets. The players responded with exponential growth. Mitchell had a combined 7-47 record over the previous two seasons. In 2012, Mitchell played for the state championship, only to lose in the final. The team's record: 23-10, with the same exact players from the lousy team the year before.

But it was the off-the-court moments Andre remembers most. Two of his players had fathers get killed in ruthless drug hits— targeted by assassins for one of the nation's most notorious drug kingpins, Craig Petties, who brought in millions of dollars' worth of coke every month from Mexico. During the season, the murder-for-hire trial played out in Memphis, a nonstop topic on the news. One hit man testified about killing people he had known for years. "It was just business," he said in federal court.

Andre and head coach Faragi Phillips talked with both players about their fathers' deaths. "We told them, 'You're going through some tragic circumstances, but are you going to sulk about it or are you going to say, 'Hey, I'm somebody like everyone else and can make the best of a bad situation.' . . . The guys stepped up to the challenge. We told them there is no success without commitment. It's about being responsible and taking responsibility."

Getting involved with the youth was something he had wanted to do but never had time for due to the constraints of professional basketball. Returning to Memphis after so many years overseas and seeing the squalor of the city year-round was sad, Andre said, but also inspiring because "it makes you want to embrace Memphis and figure out a way you can help the city become better."

Like Chris Garner, Andre knows the tragic consequences of what it's like to lose a teammate and friend. During his four years at Memphis State, Andre roomed with Baskerville Holmes, who killed his girlfriend and then himself in 1997. "I have a picture of me and him together, our arms around each other. We had just lost to Louisville in the Metro Tournament. We're there on the court, him and myself together, alone, consoling each other. We bled Tiger blue. . . . I hate how things turned out so tragically for him. Baskerville just had a huge heart.

"Every fifth of May, which was his birthday, I always think about him. I go down with a friend to his grave site and put flowers on his grave. Baskerville, he and I had a strong bond. It was just one of those things that we shared."

He said it's awesome that so many players are pitching in to change the image of Memphis basketball. The kids across the city desperately need it. The coaching outgrowth has happened organically. "All of our situations are kind of uniquely different. It wasn't a collective effort where we talked about what we're doing."

Todd Day, the all-time leading scorer at the University of Arkansas and the No. 8 pick in the NBA in 1992, began coaching five years ago in the city on the bluff. He compared the efforts by the old ballplayers to *The Blind Side,* but "in this case, it's blacks helping blacks, so it won't get as much media exposure," he joked.

"This is the same concept. You're taking care of somebody and giving love to somebody who wasn't getting taken care of at home."

He talked with Penny in recent years about coming back, but retired NBA players sometimes "don't really know what they want to do, especially for a guy like him who's made a lot of money in his career. He's one of the few privileged guys who can pretty much do whatever he wants. But he's dove into this wholeheartedly."

Todd said he and Penny work with youth to "point out positive people and negative people who don't do the right things. There's been better basketball players than Penny and myself from this area that just didn't make it for whatever reasons. So we tell them that: Just because you have talent doesn't mean you're going to make it. Most of these guys don't have fathers. That's where we step in and try to keep them on the right path. We keep them practicing, keep them away from the streets. We just try to keep them busy.

"The gangs are recruiting them as young as possible. The middle school kid will do what's called the running. A drug dealer will give them a hundred dollars to do something for them. The temptation is there. We try to make sure they have a couple dollars in their pockets, so they don't have to turn to the wrong things."

Chris Garner said he and the others try to be realistic with kids who have false dreams of going pro—that this generation of older ballplayers emphasizes the importance of using basketball to earn a college degree. "It's more just knowing that you have an opportunity for an education," he said. "You can't do anything without education. It used to be that you could graduate from high school, go to college, and just have a regular bachelor's degree. But now a master's degree is required for many jobs."

Penny's cousin LaMarcus Golden added, "We tell them: Don't let basketball use you. Use basketball to get you where you need to be in life."

In the corrupt world of basketball's underbelly, coaches in the Amateur Athletic Union—the elite summertime travel programs—often sell their best players to the highest bidders for thousands of dollars in cash, a transaction that the players don't even know takes place. Yet this group of retired players—I call them the Memphis Enforcers—is cutting into the seedy world of those exchanges. They don't need the money. They're coaching for the right reasons.

And not everyone is a retired professional athlete. Many are like Coach Dez. They see what's happening across Memphis and give everything they have to make a difference in the life of struggling teens.

At Dez's East High School, two of his boyhood friends stroll the halls. Eric Harris, who grew up in Binghampton, serves as the high school principal. Former NFL player Marcus Wimberly acts as the school's athletic director.

East has stood at the corner of Poplar and Holmes since it opened in 1948. No expense was spared. The floors were marble. The walls were adorned with oak paneling. In fact, the school was so lavish that the cost—nearly $2.5 million—was kept secret during construction. East became the school where every white family wanted their kid to attend. In June 1948, hundreds of whites crammed into a drugstore across the street to sign up their child. Yet by 1973, when the public schools began desegregation, the whites fled.

Eric Harris can count the number of white students at his school on his hand. Ninety-seven percent of the East population is black. The other 3 percent is composed mostly of Hispanics.

Part of his job is keeping apprised of gang activity. At least three East students got killed in gang violence outside of school since 2011. "I have to be well versed in gang activity.

"People think there's only one type of person who enters a gang. That's not true. There are a lot of different motivations to enter gangs, and the gang members know that," Eric said. "The typical kid might not have a good family life. The gangs make him feel loved and so he goes and joins the gang for that reason. You do have some kids who flat out like to be violent, and they figure the gang life is the best way to get that. You have kids who join out of fear, because they're afraid if they don't join they'll get an ass whupping every day.

"There is no set way. But the gangs are so diverse that they are able to target certain people and approach you in a way that it will resonate and make you seriously think about joining."

The most troubling trend is that the modern gangs prey on every kid. "When we were growing up, you could go to the Lester rec center and you were protected," he said. "Even for those in gangs, it was a neutral site." He said players like Penny and Desmond were encouraged by the gangs to do better in life. "They knew Penny and Dez had a future and could go on to college. They would say, 'You don't need to be doing this stuff we're doing.' They would literally take care of you.

"That was the unwritten rules of the street back then. A lot of people don't have that these days."

Outside the football locker room, the halls are lined with team photos over the years. I glanced into the eyes of the former players—all young guys with the gritty looks of boys trying to hold back smiles. That look of fake fierceness every football player flashes in team photos. As I looked at the photos, I'm told, "He's dead. He's dead. He's dead."

Marcus Wimberly played football at East and went on to the NFL. His neck is as thick as an oak stump. "This set the foundation that made me who I am today," he said in a locker room that stank of body odor and jockstraps. "East High gave me the opportunity to go to the University of Miami and meet various people. I wanted to come back and give others the same opportunities provided to me."

Many of his players don't have running water in their homes. Electricity doesn't always work, either. "We can have a parent-teacher conference day, and I can sit back and I won't see one parent," he said. One of his star running backs—who earned a scholarship to Vanderbilt—"is raising himself right now."

"When they come up here and you hear some of their stories, you're in awe trying to figure out how they're making it," he said. "We know the challenges the kids are going through and they know we can relate because we're from the area. We went to East; our families live in Binghampton. We try to get them to the point so they won't veer off onto the wrong path."

Three of his friends have been killed over the years; another fifteen are serving hard time for dealing drugs. "There could've been many situations when I could've gotten caught up in the situations with them, but never once would they let me get involved with that because they wanted me to succeed. That's why I say it's so different now. Nowadays, the gangs try to bring them down to their level."

He said he tells players that "if you get that burning feeling that something's not right, then stop and listen to it."

He gauges success by seeing his boys go off to college. "We want as many kids as possible to have that opportunity to go to college or to graduate. Our goal is to get one hundred percent to graduate."

What Penny and Desmond are doing at the middle school level can plant the seed to improve the boys' outlook when they reach East. "The earlier you can intervene and give them something positive, the better.

"There's a lot of people from my generation who have come back. It takes that family unit, that bonding to develop these kids. It means a lot to the community and to the kids. It shows them that there is a way out, other than dealing drugs."

Chris Garner and Dez were rivals in high school, constantly talking trash when Treadwell and East faced off. Those rivalries are over now. Chris nodded his head when asked about Penny and Dez joining forces at Lester. The two were changing attitudes of the players and the neighborhood.

"You have two guys who really love the kids, two guys who played the game as if it were their last every single time that they hit the floor. And to have them together, giving their talents and their experience to younger kids, it's unbelievable," he said.

"A lot of people put a lot of emphasis on Elvis Presley as the icon of Memphis, but I put mine on Anfernee Hardaway. . . . He's a great person and he cares about people. Anything that he can do for anybody, he will do it."

CHAPTER 19

Championship Time

Coach Dez pulled up in his black Chevy Camaro to the apartment where Reggie Green lived with his grandmother. Lester had beaten Airways and Lake County to earn a trip to the championship. They would face Fayette East, the team in the Tennessee backwoods that had beaten Lester 53–52 in the second game of the season.

"You're gonna win state MVP today," he said.

He spoke with Reggie about being the best player he ever coached, that when he started playing in sixth grade he couldn't dribble and didn't even know the rules of the game. He told Reggie how proud he was of him—that he'd gone through so much off the court and still maintained a level head. Dez told Reggie that he was sure he would perform at the highest level in the biggest game of his life. Everything they had worked for built up to this moment.

The pep talk was meant to put Reggie in the right frame of mind.

Dez knew about championships that got away. His junior year at East High, the team was loaded with talent. Several guys went on to play Division I basketball, including All-American Cedric Henderson, who starred at Memphis State and went on to play five seasons in the NBA. That East team was the overwhelming favorite to win state, but they got knocked out of the playoffs in the early rounds by an inferior team. Trailing late in the game, Desmond missed several clutch shots in the 57–50 loss. A crushing defeat, one that still stings twenty years later. Dez lay on the court with his back on the ground in disbelief. He's thought of that moment ever since, feeling he'd disappointed his teammates, the school, and the neighborhood. Coach Mosby especially. "I felt I had let him down because of all the stuff he had done for me in life. I was like 'I let Coach down.'" East High fell short of that title his senior year, although Desmond was nominated as a McDonald's High School All-American.

You don't get many second chances in life. Dez had gotten one when he defied death. And now he finally had another shot at a championship, twenty years later. He could feel it, he could smell it, he could taste it. He wanted the championship, not just for himself but for all of Binghampton. For the kids.

Dez dropped Reggie off at school and watched him walk through the front doors. He thought of everything Reggie had accomplished: going from a kid who couldn't dribble to a superstar; a boy devastated by his dad's fists into a young man with a positive attitude. Martin Luther King Jr. stared down from the school wall: "The time is right to always do what is right."

The anxiety among the players inside school was almost physical. Kobe Freeman was so nervous he nearly peed in his pants. When he walked into his first-period science class, the teacher joked, "Y'all are gonna lose." Fayette East's bigger guards had forced him into several key turnovers in their first confrontation, when Lester lost by a single point. He didn't want to let Dez and Penny down. Usually talkative and outgoing, Kobe stayed quiet. He said he kept thinking, What if we lose?

Robert Washington kept to himself, trying to rein in his emotions ahead of the big game. Reggie did the same. His grandfather, Antoine Richardson, met with him about handling the pressure of playing for the championship. Antoine couldn't help but marvel at the change he'd witnessed in his grandson in the months since Penny became coach. "When Penny came over to Lester, Reggie was being kind of a little bully," Antoine recalled. "I told him quit bullying your teammates. Come on, Reggie. I know you're bigger than everyone but you've got to slow down and listen to me before you end up in trouble or end up in this gang world. I better not see your hat all cocked to the side and stuff. Straighten your attitude up, because you weren't raised to be like that. I know you have some hurt in you coming up. . . . But that's why Penny came in, stepped in, and is helping you. Now that you see somebody's helping you, take advantage of it, son. Do what you got to do! Show the man you're a hard worker.

"If you want something, it's not going to come easy, Reggie. I told him that all the time: Come on and be a diehard and be a good worker and good things will come to you," Antoine continued. "And I told Reggie before we went to that game: 'Here's what I need you to do. I need you playing down low. I want you to put it on them—show me what you got! I just want to see you playing a helluva game because this is for the money.'"

Across town, Penny prepared for a feast. As the team headed toward the championship, he hosted them for dinner before every game. Tonight the dinner would be baked chicken, spaghetti, candied yams, and corn bread. The night before, Penny and Dez stayed up late talking about the big game. They wanted to make sure they would win. Penny was concerned by the size of Fayette East's guards. Some stood close to 6 feet tall. Even the smaller ones were about 5-7 and physically thick. Penny wasn't sure if

Nick, at 4-feet-11, could handle the pressure. Dez sought to calm him, saying his son had played in an AAU national title and that his experience would prove more valuable than his height.

When school let out, Dez drove the boys to Penny's house. They held hands, bowed their heads, and said the Lord's Prayer. Many sat at the large round dinner table. Others ate at an elevated bar area. The rest sat outside on the patio, looking at his magnificent swimming pool. There was no goofing off this day. Everyone knew what was at stake.

Penny reminded them that they represented all of Binghampton and had a chance to do something no other small school in Memphis had accomplished. When the team finished eating, players scattered to various rooms to rest and relax. In the movie lounge, Penny and Dez played the 2005 movie *Coach Carter*. In the film, based on a true story, Coach Ken Carter (played by Samuel L. Jackson) returns to his former high school to coach inner-city boys. He arrives to a team of punks, but Coach Carter instills rigid rules, asks for teachers to show him progress reports—and, ultimately, sees players unite and pull together in a run to the state playoffs. "Just because you deserve this doesn't mean they're going to give it to you," Coach Carter tells the team. "Sometimes you've got to take what's yours. You ready to do this?"

But the team loses in dramatic fashion at the buzzer. Seeing the disappointment in the locker room, Coach Carter downplays the outcome of the game and emphasizes what has transpired through the course of the season. "What you've achieved is that ever-elusive victory from within. And, gentlemen, I am so proud of you," he says. "I came to coach basketball players and you became students. I came to coach boys and you became men."

Dez and others around Binghampton had begun calling Penny "Coach Carter" due to his strict rules. The parallels were eerily similar. Every Lester player struggled with his home situation. They'd caused trouble throughout the season. But in the end, each had improved his grades and rallied around the others.

The movie was powerful and all, but Penny and Dez sought a different outcome. Settling for second wasn't an option.

In Binghampton, smoke from barbecue grills at Howze Park drifted across the neighborhood. Five school buses were parked at Lester to transport fans from the neighborhood to the game. Robert Washington's aunt—and his grandmother, siblings, cousins, all his uncles—prepared for the ride. The Memphis Duck could hardly contain himself. And inside prison, Reggie Green's dad awaited word on the outcome.

When Dez drove up in the team van with the players, it became a party atomosphere: bass-booming music, rival gangs high-fiving, moms and grandmas cheering for their boys. In the van, the boys remained silent, listening to their iPods, gifts Penny had given each player at Christmas.

Dez mashed the van's accelerator and the Binghampton entourage was off to Geeter Middle School, about twenty minutes south of downtown, in Whitehaven.

It was game time.

CHAPTER 20

Championships That Got Away

The land of Disney wanted something real, something more tangible than the make-believe that engulfs the city of Orlando. The folks there were tired of Mickey Mouse and his empire. They wanted to dunk-face Cinderella.

The combination of Shaquille O'Neal and Penny Hardaway made the reality of an NBA championship come to life for the Orlando Magic. Any doubt, any animosity that fans once had toward Penny over the trade for Chris Webber had been erased. Management's decision to go after the kid from Memphis rather than the more hyped member of Michigan's Fab Five proved to be prophetic. The Magic compiled a 57–25 record in the 1995 regular season to sit atop the Eastern Conference. Banners around the city read: "Why not us? Why not now?"

And why not? The starting lineup was rounded out by Nick Anderson, the first player the franchise picked when the team was formed in 1989; three-point specialist Dennis Scott; and Horace Grant, who had been brought in for his veteran leadership from the Chicago Bulls, where he won three championships with Michael Jordan and Scottie Pippen.

The Magic blew through the first round of the playoffs, beating the Boston Celtics 3-1 in a five-game series. They followed with a tough matchup against Jordan and the Bulls. With the series tied 2-2, the Magic won the next two games to eliminate Chicago, including a 108–102 victory in Chicago to clinch. Penny poured in 21 points and dished out 7 assists in that game—a sign that the mantle of the NBA's next Hall of Fame guard was being passed from Jordan to Penny.

"We grew up," Penny, then twenty-three, told reporters.

The Indiana Pacers pushed the young Magic team to the brink in the Eastern Conference Finals. The Magic held a 3-2 series edge and traveled to Indianapolis with a chance to earn the franchise's first trip to the NBA Finals. Reggie Miller had other plans. He lit up the Magic for 36 points and got in Penny's head, holding him to just 11. The Pacers embarrassed the Magic, 123–96, to force a Game 7 in Orlando. Penny and Dennis Scott huddled the team after the game and told everyone to look at the scoreboard—to never forget how badly they had been beaten. Back in Orlando for Game 7, the Magic was determined not to disappoint the hometown crowd. The first half was tight with Orlando leading 52–45, but the Magic soon pulled away, ripping the Pacers, 105–81. Shaq threw down 25 points; Penny added 17.

"Everybody kept saying we couldn't shoot free throws, we didn't have the experience, we couldn't go all the way," Penny told reporters. "It motivated us, it really did. While everybody was criticizing, we just kept playing ball."

The stage was set. The Magic would square off against the defending NBA champion Houston Rockets, an experienced team led by Hakeem Olajuwon, Clyde Drexler, and Kenny Smith. The Rockets were a sixth seed coming into the playoffs and written off as too old, too slow. But they gained momentum, first beating the 60-22 Utah Jazz, then the 59-23 Phoenix Suns, and finally the league's best team, the 62-20 San Antonio Spurs. If they were to win the championship, Houston would become the first team in NBA history to beat four fifty-win teams.

Orlando was psyched.

It was June 7, 1995, the first time the city ever hosted an NBA championship game. The year before, Penny had attended Game 1 in Houston when the Rockets played the New York Knicks. "I remember players coming by, winking at me and saying, 'Don't you wish you were here?'" he said. "Now, it's my turn to smile and wink."

The Orlando Arena was jammed with 16,010 frenetic fans who sent the noise-o-meter into overdrive. They waved white rally rags that the organization handed out at the gate. One sign held by fans scrolled nearly an entire row. It had X's through the Celtics, Bulls, Pacers, and Rockets. "Magic 1995 champs," it read.

Another sign said, "Watch for falling Rockets."

The O-rena, as it was called, bounced with excitement. The Magic held home-court advantage, another sure reason to believe that this was their year. Orlando was unstoppable in the place: an unbelievable 46-4. In the Magic locker room, forward Horace Grant showed off the three NBA championship rings he won with the Chicago Bulls. "It's a helluva combination of rings," said Magic forward Donald Royal.

The pregame hype billed the Shaq-Olajuwon duel as one of the greatest matchups of centers since Bill Russell and Wilt Chamberlain played in the 1960s. Olajuwon had bested Shaq in the regular season, averaging 23.8 points, 10.8 rebounds, and 4.2 blocks to Shaq's 20.7 points, 12.8 rebounds, and 1.7 blocks. "He can do it all—left side, right side," O'Neal said. "He has a complete game."

The NBC telecast began with a glitzy pregame montage pitting the two teams against each other like it was the battle for a boxing heavyweight title. "The Orlando Magic were labeled too immature, too inexperienced to contend for a title this year. It's too soon they were told," said Bob Costas as video flashed up monster dunks by Shaq.

The sharply produced video went straight to an interview with Shaq. "At the beginning of the season, I looked at the projected starting five: Horace, Nick, D. Scott, Penny, myself. And I said, 'We can do it.'"

The video then cut back to Costas, who, in his silky-smooth delivery, said, "And so far, they have done it. Orlando has simply turned the clock ahead. Their party starts now. Tonight the reigning champs versus the precocious challengers."

It was game time.

Now live, Costas turned toward the camera, his hair perfectly coiffed as it always was. "The story here is this: The Orlando Magic is universally regarded as the NBA's team of the future. There are almost certainly championships ahead for Shaquille O'Neal, Anfernee Hardaway, and company. The question is: Can the Rockets make them wait a little longer? Maybe not, because with each passing game the Magic seem even more resourceful, more sure of themselves, their youth no longer such an obstacle."

Right from the tip-off, Penny came out on fire. He had averaged 29 points a game against Houston during the regular season and was well on his way to reaching that mark in this game. He had four inches on Houston's Kenny Smith, and Penny took full advantage. He took him inside. He drained a fadeaway. He got a breakaway dunk. With 3:31 left in the first quarter, Penny pump-faked, froze Smith, and scored another bucket, getting fouled in the process. Shaq had picked up two early fouls. Penny put the team on his back, scoring 11 points in the opening frame. Orlando led 30–19 at the end of the first quarter.

The Magic didn't let up. They stretched the lead to 20 on a

three-pointer by Nick Anderson, making the score 57–37. The crowd waved white rally towels in the air: This was their moment. Yes! The Magic is gonna cream these old guys and send them packing back to Houston. Who cares what the NBA experts had to say? The young guns were ready. This was the Magic's time!

Feeding off Penny's electric play, Nick Anderson played like nobody's business. He kept shooting and hitting. He poured in 15 points in the first half. The Rockets were on the ropes. They couldn't break through. The Magic was too tough, the crowd too boisterous. They couldn't be silenced.

But Clyde Drexler—who had come to Houston from Portland in a bold trade to try to get him his first championship—managed to keep the Rockets within arm's reach, cutting the lead to 61–50 at the half after most of the Magic's starters had subbed out.

Olajuwon had said "never underestimate the heart of a lion," and he took over in the third quarter. "Olajuwon, yes!" NBC announcer Marv Albert said after a skyhook that began a massive run. That bucket trimmed the score to 61–54. A few minutes later, Houston had stormed all the way back, to trail just 67–66. The O-rena drew quiet. *Stunned* was the only apropos word. The Rockets outscored the Magic 37–19, fueled by Olajuwon's dominance of Shaq and Kenny Smith's three-pointers. They stretched their lead.

Houston 87, Orlando 80 at the end of three.

The veterans had put the upstarts—or in Costas's lingo *the precocious challengers*—in place. The arena, so animated, so loud earlier in the game, grew completely quiet. Worried fans placed both hands on their heads in disbelief at what had transpired. The Magic's lead didn't just disappear, it went up in a poof of smoke. The fourth quarter began with each team continuing to battle. The fans were back in the game, trying their best to rally the home team, to spur on the Magic. The crowd rained down chants of "Defense! Defense!" An organist chimed in with tunes to further pump up the team. Gradually the Magic began a comeback. Trailing 96–95 with under seven minutes to go, they gave the ball to Penny. He eyed the basket from three-point land and let it sail.

Bingo!

"And for Hardaway, his first three-pointer," Marv Albert said. "He missed his previous five."

The crowd stood, getting louder with each possession. But Houston didn't hesitate. They pushed the ball quickly up court and found Olajuwon on the baseline. He gave a hitch move, hooked around, and caught Shaq sleeping on defense to tie the game, 98–98. The game continued at a frenetic back-and-forth pace.

With the teams knotted at 102, Brian Shaw tossed a no-look pass to a streaking Shaq, who powered the ball home. "Hakeem was running just as fast as he could, and could not even gain a stride on him," NBC commentator Bill Walton said. "Nothing anybody could do. The Big Man finishing!"

With 1:17 left and Orlando clinging to a 108–107 lead, Shaq answered the call again. He gave an up-and-under fake for yet another bucket: Orlando 110, Houston 107. The Rockets could not convert. The Magic held the ball. The fat lady was singing. The game for all intents and purposes was over. The seconds ticked off the clock, seemingly in slow motion. With less than fifteen seconds, the Magic went into a four-corners stall mode to run out the clock and take this victory to the locker room. The O-rena grew deafening, everyone standing, cheering, stomping, high-fiving.

It was the Magic moment the city had long awaited. "Foul called with 10.5 seconds to go," Marv Albert said.

The Rockets fouled Nick Anderson, a fan favorite because he was the guy whom the Magic built the franchise around, the first player ever to don a Magic uniform. He'd endured some wretched seasons during those fledgling years. It was fitting he would be the one to seal the deal this night. He had gotten less of the spotlight ever since Shaq and Penny had arrived. A 67 percent free throw shooter for the year, Nick stepped up to the line.

MAKE ROOM FOR ANDERSON IN NEXT FRAME, a headline in the *St. Petersburg Times* read that morning.

"This is the way it works for Nick Anderson," the article declared. "No matter what he does, it seems he's always in the middle of someone else's story. Remember that stranger between the camera and Aunt Martha in your vacation photos? That was Anderson."

The Magic bench stood—Brian Shaw, Jeff Turner, Anthony Bowie, Donald Royal. Coach Brian Hill squatted near the scorer's table.

Clank.

The ball hit the front of the rim with such a heavy thud it echoed over the screams and wails of distraught fans. It was a noise that couldn't be replicated even if you tried.

But it happened, again.

Clank.

The second free throw hit the same exact spot, made the same appalling noise, and then bounced wildly through the arms of Kenny Smith and right back into the hands of Nick Anderson.

"Anderson missing on both," Marv Albert said, "but gets to the rebound and again draws the foul." Nick sat on the floor for a couple of seconds after the foul, his legs straight in front of him. Shaq leaned over, whispered something in his ear, and helped him off the ground.

There were 7.9 seconds left.

Now, the O-rena's 16,010 drew so quiet it was almost like they already knew what would happen next. Nick reluctantly stepped back up to the line. This time the ball arched through the air and off the back of the rim. Exasperated, Nick turned his back to the goal and snapped his head, shouting "Damn!" to no one in particular.

He was now 12 of 17 on free throws this night, 71 percent. Surely, he wouldn't miss four consecutive free throws. The fourth shot hit the back of the rim, sputtering awkwardly up in the air and off the backboard, before bouncing off the front of the rim. "And he misses four straight," Marv Albert said.

Shaq crashed the boards and swiped the ball backward—to try to get it to one of his teammates. The ball landed in the hands of Kenny Smith for the Rockets. He immediately called a time-out. Nick Anderson twirled his body and looked straight up at the arena's roof, in anger, in disbelief, in disgust. An indelible image of a man in defeat.

It would still take a miracle for the Rockets to tie the game. The score remained Orlando 110, Houston 107. With 5.6 seconds left, the Rockets threw the ball in to Kenny Smith. He had already connected on six three-pointers this night. He faked toward the basket, catching Penny off guard, and then stepped back and let fly another three-pointer from the top of the key.

"He's been on fire," Marv said as the ball hung in the air. "And hits! He's tied the game at 110!" NBC color commentator Bill Walton added, "Kenny Smith says forget it."

Smith's seven three-pointers set an NBA Finals record. The Magic tried to put it behind them. They hung tough in overtime, matching the Rockets every step of the way. But with the score knotted 118–118 with 5.5 seconds left, Clyde Drexler streaked down the right side of the lane.

"Drexler driving. He goes. He puts it up," said NBA Radio announcer Joe McConnell. "Oh the rebound! Tipped in! Tipped in! By Hakeem! The Houston Rockets have stunned the Orlando Magic."

The Rockets sprinted off the court, their arms raised in jubilation, rushing to their locker room as fast as they could. Olajuwon finished with 31 points. Kenny Smith added 23. The 16,010 fans stood in a daze, their eyes blinking as if trying to block out the image of what just transpired.

Penny, Shaq, Nick Anderson—the entire team—walked off the court and through the corridor without saying a word. The silence continued into the locker room.

The Magic's fate was sealed. They got swept and never recovered—not even to this day. Nick Anderson became vilified in Orlando, even though he remains the franchise's all-time leading scorer. Fans dubbed him Nick the Brick and Brick Anderson. His play suffered. He couldn't shoot free throws anymore. At one point, his free throw percentage plummeted to 36 percent.

In 2009, NBA.com writer Fran Blinebury ranked the four missed free throws as one of the most pivotal moments in the history of a sports franchise—because the dynasty that was to become the Orlando Magic got obliterated: "One night, one game, one simple shot that changed a franchise and maybe the face of professional basketball in the 1990s and beyond."

It's a memory that still haunts the players and coaches.

"If he makes one free throw out of four, then we're not talking anymore," said Buzz Braman, Orlando's shooting coach. "We'd have gone on and won a ring.

"It was an awful, awful, awful scene. Everybody was shell-shocked in that locker room. I'll never forget it, because literally nobody could say anything. That should've been a team that was together for another five or six years. I think everybody figured we would be back. We were that good. And they never got back."

Nearly twenty years later Braman still ponders the what-ifs—the Magic goes on to win the series, Shaq never leaves, the Magic becomes one of the most talked-about teams in NBA history. Maybe Penny never gets hurt, maybe he never undergoes the botched knee surgeries that ruined his career.

"He would've been remembered as an athletic Magic Johnson."

But life moves on.

Dwelling on what-ifs gets you nowhere. Penny said the Magic was supposed to take a delay of game before Kenny Smith's game-tying three-pointer in regulation, but it didn't happen. That "made me late on going out on Kenny Smith," Penny said. "The only reason he got that three is because I relaxed.

"I would tell the younger Penny, you should've done more—to go on and win it. That way every time you look at the highlights, you'll be the winner and not the loser," Penny said, laughing. "It is what it is. When you're young, you're going to go through experiences and that's the best teacher."

Penny said if he had his way, the starters would never have sat out after they built the 20-point lead in the first half. "We should've just smashed them all the way out and took all their confidence and then beat them in Game One. Then, who knows what would've gone on. We were the better team. We just got our confidence shattered and then they got their confidence up. . . . Everything just went their way from when they made the run at the end of the first half all the way until the game ended."

He added, "Getting swept was embarrassing. History is history, though." Despite it all, Penny said, "I loved playing with Horace, Nick, Shaq, and Dennis. Those guys were amazing. I was in awe, and I was a fan of all those guys."

As the Lester Lions prepared for their own title, Penny didn't need a reminder about the championships that get away. He had lived it.

CHAPTER 21

The Final Game

Silence consumed the locker room. Everything the boys had worked for or on—the conditioning drills, the improved schoolwork, the bonds of brotherhood—came down to this. A rematch with Fayette East, the team that beat Lester early in the season. Revenge was on the minds of each player, but so was anxiety.

Coach Penny told them throughout the season that to be the best, you had to beat the best. This was the carpe diem moment, to prove they had the heart of lions, like the emblem on their uniforms. Reggie, Robert, Nick, Kobe—all the players—slipped on their black jerseys with gold trim.

Coach Dez carried with him a Bible that Rev. Larry Peoples gave him when he was hospitalized. He opened the book to Psalms 23:4. He gathered his composure before reading the highlighted verse.

Yea, though I walk through the valley of the shadow of death,
I will fear no evil;
For You are with me;
Your rod and Your staff, they comfort me.

It was the same verse his high school coach, Reginald Mosby, read to the East High Mustangs before games. But Dez now knew what the verse meant. He'd walked through the valley of death and survived. He feared nothing. Dez thought of Coach Mosby and the lessons he instilled in him as a young man—the locker room chats in which Coach Mosby comforted Dez about not having a father in his life.

Dez looked up from his Bible, his voice catching, unable to find the appropriate words to speak with the team. His son, Nick, choked up and fought back his tears, too. None of the other players said anything. They simply stared at Coach. More than anything, they wanted to capture the title for Dez.

Penny told the team that the last few months had come down to this. The Final Game. They set a goal of winning the state from the outset and now it was time to conquer. Were they going to man up or wilt?

Kobe and Reggie asked the team, including Dez and Penny, to gather round in prayer. They thanked God for getting them to this point, asked Him to give the team strength, to guide them. The players locked arms and ended, as they always did, with the team's chant. "All for one! One for all! All for Lester!"

A month earlier, Penny had questioned the players' attitudes when the season threatened to slip away: Did that chant mean anything to them? Were they too selfish to comprehend it? Why hadn't they shown him that they cared about one another as teammates, as friends, as brothers?

Now he stepped back and cherished the moment. The man who grew up without a dad had become surrogate father to the dozen boys in the room. In just three months, he'd shown them love like no one else. They wanted to prove to Coach Penny that they had what it took—that they wouldn't disappoint.

The Lester Lions rushed onto the court to the team's rap song.

King of the jungle
Yeah, I'm a Lion
Super fly swag
You can say my flag's flying
Yeah, I'm a Lion

It seemed all of Binghampton was crammed into the gym. Their fans outnumbered Fayette East's by about 10 to 1. Bozo Williams darted onto the floor, grooving his hips and energizing the crowd.

"We are the Lions! Mighty, mighty Lions!" the fans chanted.

Reggie's grandfather Antoine Richardson sat right behind the team. "I just want you to play a helluva game," he told his grandson.

Reggie looked up in the stands and saw his mother. She didn't come to many games, but no matter what, he never stopped loving her. He blew her a kiss.

It was time.

Wayne Jackson sat amid the purple of the Fayette East Bulldog fans. Wayne is about 6-6 and built like a refrigerator. His son, DJ, a big-bodied 6-3 power forward, starred for Fayette East and stood poised to be the state MVP as a seventh grader.

"Let's whup Penny," Wayne said.

And right out of the gate, Fayette East sought to do just that. Lester's specialty was to jump on teams at tip-off, intimidate with their speed, and build insurmountable leads. Fayette East was having none of it. Penny's concern about Lester's smaller guards proved to be legit. The Bulldogs' guards controlled the game early on, pushing the pace and forcing turnover after turnover. It was 14–6 within the first three minutes, and Lester didn't have an answer. Kobe came off the bench and brought some poise to the team. Lester soon went on an 8–2 run to get back in the game. It was a game of runs.

At quarter's end, Fayette East led 16–14.

Penny and Dez huddled the team. Penny praised them for clawing back but told them not to let up. They needed to stay composed and play their game. Nick Merriweather immediately stole the ball to start the second quarter and quickly passed up court to Courtney McLemore, who dished to a racing Reggie Green for a layup to knot the score at 16. The Lions showed they could storm back and hang with the larger, more physical country boys.

It didn't last.

The Bulldogs dominated the next two minutes. They went on a 10–4 run, shutting down Reggie and Robert in the paint and preventing Lester's guards from getting open shots. The score stood at 26–20 in the closing seconds of the half, in favor of Fayette East. The Bulldogs harassed Nick as he dribbled up the floor. He struggled to get the ball past half-court and threw the ball erratically to Courtney, who nearly turned the ball over. The Bulldog guards were more like pit bulls, jumping on top of the small Lester players, forcing them into traps, imposing their will. Lester tried to hold the ball for the final shot of the half, but when Courtney got the ball back on the left wing and tried to hit Nick with a pass at the top of the key, it was immediately stolen. A Fayette East guard stormed to the basket—little Nick Merriweather tumbling to the ground trying to stop him—and scooped in a layup for a 28–20 lead. Lester tried a desperation three-pointer before the clock ran out, but to no avail. The Lions trailed by eight at the half.

Penny held his chin high in the locker room. Dressed in a navy blazer and silver tie, he personified class and dignity. He looked at the group of dejected faces. Reggie sat with his head between his legs. Robert had a stunned look of disbelief. Fayette East was too strong, too fast, too big. DJ Jackson had clawed Robert on the inside, pounded him any time the ball came to him.

Penny calmed them, said they still had a second half to play. He reminded them that Lester players don't quit, that they fight to the end. That they were playing not just for themselves but for all of Binghampton.

Fayette East pounced on the Lions' tentative play to start the second half. "You can take that to yo' momma," one Fayette East guard told Nick after hitting a three in his face.

The Bulldogs stretched the lead to 34–25, before pulling away even further, to a commanding 16-point lead. The score stood at 45–32 at the end of the third. And by the fourth quarter, the Lester fans, so jubilant, so wild, so loud at the start of the game, were silent. Fayette East continued to pull away, building a 47–32 lead. Nick and Courtney passed the ball back and forth around mid-court, as if neither wanted to handle the ball. Nick inched his way to the top of the key. The defenders backed off. Nick hesitated at first. Then the smallest kid on the floor let the ball fly.

Swish!

"There you go!" Antoine Richardson shouted.

But Fayette East countered with a quick bucket—the dagger—to take a 49–35 lead with just over five minutes to play. The teams traded buckets over the next minute at a frenetic pace. The fat lady was tuning her voice. Because this game was done. The back-water boys were sending the boys in the Hood back crying. It was game over. Lights out.

Penny called time-out in frustration—and desperation. The game was getting away from him and the boys. Reggie and Robert hung their heads. The guards had looks of surrender. "I saw that if we just gained our composure for a couple minutes, then we could make a run if we made the shots," Penny recalled later. "When they came to the bench, they were all disappointed, disgusted, and frustrated. . . . I'm thinking we'll walk out of here with our heads up."

The looks of defeat stood against everything Penny had instilled in them:

- You can overcome your circumstances.
- Always dream big.
- Fight through pain.

With the team huddled, Penny told them that a strong effort to finish would allow Lester to leave with their pride intact, even if they lost. "Just give me all you got," he said.

It wasn't supposed to be this way. Lester had ridden an eleven-game winning streak into the championship for a 22-3 record. Yet the Hollywood script—*Local Legend Returns to Bring Memphis School First Title*—was being torn up. The Coach Carter nickname was becoming all too real; Penny would lose another championship.

Binghampton fans who had boasted about Penny before tip-off started leaving the gym. Reggie's grandfather Antoine sought to quell the rebellion. "Y'all are fixing to miss something special!" he hollered. "These kids can hit threes. Please, don't leave!"

Wayne Jackson put on his Fayette East jacket and swelled out his barrel chest. His son DJ had scored 16 points and had the state MVP wrapped up. "It's 'nah-nah-nah-nah good-bye' time!"

Coach David Ayers, whose Lara Kendall team had lost to Lester in the semifinals, noticed how angry the Lester fans were getting. Their notorious reputation was well-known, even in his country town, one hundred miles north of Memphis, near the Kentucky border. People were stomping up and down the sidelines, screaming and yelling and cussing. He didn't want to get caught in a riot. The gangsters were getting restless.

"It's time to go," he told his kids.

"You hear the stories about Lester and the guys that hang around," he recalled. "That's why we left."

The Lester players weren't immune to what was transpiring. Robert was in a daze. He was getting overpowered by DJ Jackson. He stared into the stands at the fans leaving and dropped his head. "Hold your damn head up," said Auntie Shree.

Reggie wanted to cry, but sucked it up like a man. He looked at Coach Penny and the rest of his team in the huddle. Nick struggled to keep in his emotions. He was one of Lester's most experienced players, having played since he was seven. Yet Penny's fears that Fayette East's guards would shut him down had proved to be true.

"Look, do not give up on me," Penny shouted in the huddle.

He considered pulling Nick. He was outmatched in height, weight, and speed. Lester fans felt the same. "Put Kobe in!" they screamed.

Penny's gut told him to stick with Nick. He told the team to get it down low to Reggie or Robert, and then pass it to an open guard for a three-pointer. The team that had struggled in clutch time all year was now being asked to do the unthinkable—charge back from an overwhelming deficit.

"Just give me all you got," Penny repeated one last time.

The dozen boys put their hands on top of Coach Penny's. "One for all! All for one! All for Lester!" they shouted.

Fayette East panicked coming out of the time-out. Instead of attacking the basket, they went into a stall mode. It's always a risky strategy, even at the highest level. Players have a tendency to tense up. They think more about the seconds ticking away, rather than the game itself. Asking middle school kids to try to hold the ball wasn't just risky; it was foolish.

Reggie stole the ball. He pushed it up court and found an open guard, Demarcus "Black" Martin, who let sail another three-pointer.

Swish!

The Fayette East coach should have called a time-out and calmed his players, but instead they stayed on the court and freaked. Reggie seized the moment and pounced on another loose ball. He got it to Nick, who fired another three.

Swish!

The gym sounded like the roof blew off. This time, Nick swirled his fingers an extra few seconds and let them dance in the air. It was his way of talking smack: I'm in the zone. And just like that, Lester was chipping away: 53–43. Coach Dez struggled to stand. He clapped and pumped his fist. What had seemed nearly insurmountable suddenly seemed possible.

The ball came back to Demarcus for another three-pointer.

Swish!

The inbounds pass was lobbed into the middle of the court. Courtney McLemore grabbed it and found Nick. He planted his feet and fired from twenty-two feet away. The tiniest of kids showed he had the biggest heart.

Swish!

Another three-pointer. The team's fourth three-pointer in a minute and a half. Nick glanced at his father on the bench and smiled a toothy grin—the type of look Dez always wanted to give when he played ball.

Lester called a time-out to go for the jugular. Reggie chest-bumped Nick. Penny sought calm. The Bulldogs' lead had been trimmed to 53–49.

"We got them now," Penny shouted. "This is our time."

The Lester contingent screamed, *"Defense! Defense!"* Bozo Williams gestured for them to stand up, to yell at the top of their lungs.

"Binghampton, stand up!" Antoine Richardson yelled.

Fayette East threw the ball inbounds. Their guard dribbled up court into a trap. Lester players were on him like a lion on an antelope. Black ended up with the ball and passed to Reggie, who powered in for a layup to cut the lead to 53–51 with just over two minutes left. The defense tightened. Fayette East missed its next shot, and Reggie grabbed the rebound and got fouled.

Reggie blocked out everything. He walked to the free throw line and nailed both to tie the score, 53–53, with fifty seconds left. It was the closest Lester had come to leading in the game since tip-off. Fayette East coughed up the ball again. Black passed to Reggie down low. He faked left and went right. He soared in the air, cradled the ball, and scooped it up and under for a reverse layup. The ball kissed the glass and went in: 55–53, Lester's first lead.

"Oooooh, boy!" his grandfather shouted. "I ain't seen that before. You're showing me something tonight!"

Still, the game wasn't sealed. A Fayette East player drove to the basket and tied the score with 23.7 seconds remaining. Courtney got fouled on the next possession and made one of two free throws to give Lester a 56–55 edge. Fayette East had a chance to hold the ball for the final shot to win, but a DJ Jackson pass went off the hands of a teammate and out of bounds. The Bulldogs immediately fouled Demarcus with fifteen seconds remaining. If he made both, the game was virtually over. Lester would have a three-point lead, and the worst that could happen would be overtime. His hands trembled. Demarcus stood at the free throw line.

"Missssssssssss!" Fayette East fans hissed.

Clank.

Penny motioned for him to calm down, to take a deep breath. On the second attempt, the ball left his fingertips and arced through the air. It seemed like slow motion. The ball bounced off the back of the rim. In that moment, time froze. Robert Washington leaped like a beast and used his 7-foot wingspan to snag the rebound. He put the ball off the glass for a 58–55 lead with eight seconds left. A stunned Fayette East called time-out. DJ Jackson buried his head in a towel.

On the sideline, Coach Dez had tears rolling down his cheeks. Of all the people who sparked the comeback, it was his son, Nick.

But the game was far from over. A three-pointer could still tie the game and force overtime. The Lester fans rose to their feet. It sounded like a fifteen-thousand-seat arena, their chants of "Defense! Defense!" reverberating off the hardwood.

Fayette East was shell-shocked. A gigantic lead blown. They needed a three-pointer to tie the game, but they didn't even attempt one. Amid the team's daze as the seconds wound down, a Fayette East guard drove to the basket for a layup to make it 58–57 as the buzzer sounded.

Lester Middle School had won the West Tennessee State Title, 58–57. By a penny.

"Everything we had gone through with school, in practice, in games, it probably ranks one or two" in my all-time highlights, Penny said afterward. "Honestly, because it was out of my control. Every other game has been in my control because I've been a part of it as a player. But standing on the sideline, I couldn't help them make a shot. I couldn't help them play defense."

Dez said, "That just showed the heart and the courage that these kids have in this neighborhood. They never gave up. Being down fifteen points with three minutes left, I don't know anybody who wouldn't have stopped playing and acting like the game was over. But they never gave up. . . . We never saw anything like that in life."

The fans of Binghampton rushed the court. The team piled on top of one another. Reggie, Robert, Kobe, and Nick cried in celebration. Robert's aunt joined in the pile, hugging all the boys. Dez couldn't utter a word. He wrapped his arms around Nick and held him tight. His son had given him the greatest reward. "He's small but he's a fighter," Dez said later. "He just got that feeling that we're fixing to lose. He had seen me go through what I went through. He took it upon himself. The bulb just clicked on at the right time."

Penny stood at center court. If smiles were contagious on his first day of practice, tears were infectious this night. "All we went through together this year as a team, it was incredible," Penny recalled. "I saw Dez crying. I saw a couple players crying. I was like 'Oh, man, don't do it.'" Penny wiped the tears from his eyes and looked up. His grandmother was with him, even in her absence. "If you want to get somewhere you've never been, you've got to do something you've never done," she had told him years before.

"God, you are amazing," Penny said.

Each player received a medal for winning the championship. Coach Dez and Penny were awarded a three-foot-tall trophy. It was debatable who earned the state MVP. Reggie had 20 points, 13 rebounds, 3 steals, and 2 blocks; Robert finished with 18 points, 14 rebounds, and 6 blocks.

The award went to Reggie, just as Dez had predicted. Reggie clutched the plaque in both arms and closed his eyes.

"I'm not gonna lie," Reggie said later. "I thought we were gonna lose, but the guards kept hitting. Penny was like 'Just play your game.' I was fixing to start crying. We've never been down like that. We had our heads down. He was like 'Y'all put your heads up.'"

Kobe added, "We all smiled and some of us cried, because this was our last game."

In the locker room, the boys coddled the trophy like it was the prized NBA crown, running their fingers across it and holding it above their heads. Dez was too overwhelmed to address the team. Penny did all the talking.

"This game isn't the end," he said. "I'm gonna be in your lives forever now."

Reggie, Robert, Kobe, Nick—the whole team—were stunned. They figured Penny would move on. "When he said, 'I'm going to be with you for the rest of your life,' I couldn't believe it. I just smiled," Reggie said. "We thought it was just for the season. But he's gonna be with us for good. He said, 'We're family now.'"

"After the game, when I was thinking about my daddy, that's when Penny said he was in my life forever now."

"Even if we hadn't won the state," Penny recalled, "it was a one hundred percent success because we touched a lot of kids. Winning the state was just the cherry on top. It was like unscrambling a puzzle and putting a puzzle together. When you finally finish it, you're proud. You look back and say, 'Wow, I worked really hard and I was a piece of that puzzle.' And we'll always be a part of each other's lives. Because winning the state, those kids will never forget it, and me and Desmond will never forget it."

When Penny finished the locker room speech, he and Dez walked across the court. The lights glistened off the hardwood as they made their way to the door. It was similar to four months earlier, when they left the charity game together. That night was about reminiscing and uniting. Tonight was something greater. They pushed the door open. A sea of Lester fans erupted in cheers.

"Binghampton, stand up!" they hooted.

Penny and Dez raised their hands. Together, they had earned their first championship.

The state champion Lester Lions. Front row, left to right: Kobe "Mayor" Freeman (1), Nick Merriweather (3), Demarcus "Black" Martin (5). Middle row: Coach Desmond Merriweather, Andrew Murphy (13), Albert Zleh (14), Derrick Carnes (10), Courtney McLemore (4), Robert Washington (20), Reggie Green (24), George Bee (12), Coach LaMarcus Golden. Back row: Penny Hardaway and Xavier Young (22, mostly hidden). The final player Alex Lomax (2) wasn't present.

Reggie Green played in front of his grandmother's apartment one Friday evening. A few older teens hung out on the nearby corner. A car circled the street and then slowed to a crawl. A gangster rolled down the window and sprayed bullets. A kid from Douglass High School was killed and three others were wounded.

"They were just shooting like this right here," Reggie's grandma Sheila Harris said, waving her index finger across the room. "Who do I see running across, but Reginald? I panicked.

"I wish you could spend the night around here to see what I'm talking about. There's some shit that goes on around here and you'd probably be like, How the fuck can you raise your child up in here?"

His grandma said the family forgave Reggie's father for beating him so severely, and she makes sure Reggie stays in contact by writing his dad weekly letters. "As far as the beating and whatever that came about, you know, it's about growing up and being a father to a child," she said.

In a brief phone conversation from prison, Taz expressed remorse, said how sorry he was. "I love that boy," Taz told me. The phone then dropped.

Along those lines, Penny and Desmond formed a group they call Fathers to help imprisoned dads from Binghampton stay connected to their children. A convicted cocaine and marijuana dealer, serving four years in a Kentucky prison, told me he's been incarcerated for the last thirty months and missed key moments of his daughter's life as she blossomed from a nine-year-old girl to an emerging track star at twelve. Penny and Desmond have helped guys like him stay united with their kids. "It's so hard to be locked up and not be there, to be as supportive as I want to be," he said. "Having guys like Desmond and Penny step in and be the mediator for us for our children—that's real important, to keep us con-

Epilogue

More than a thousand residents of Binghampton took part in a parade to celebrate the championship. Not only did Lester win the middle school title but East High School captured the Tennessee state title, too.

After the parades and celebrations, the boys of Lester returned to classes and finished out the school year. With basketball done, life pressed on.

nected with our children, to show them that we still love them, even though we're not there."

Nick Merriweather, Robert Washington, Demarcus "Black" Martin, and Kobe Freeman show off the awards the Lions won in the 2012 season.

The lessons Penny and Desmond have instilled in the boys of Lester, he said, extend far beyond the basketball court. "It's an awesome thing for Binghampton as a whole. It's like a panacea—a healing process for the whole community, for Penny to come back and say, 'You too can make it.' Dez and Penny, they're just all-around genuine, good people. Those two guys are priceless souls."

Robert Washington grew another two inches over the summer. When he wasn't playing basketball, he was holed up in his aunt's home. Auntie Shree said she was having to keep a close eye on girls pursuing him—after all, that's what happens when you get tagged with the label of potential superstar.

Kobe Freeman prepared for high school with new enthusiasm and a more upbeat outlook on life. "Last year Dez fell off and we were upset, but he came back. And this year we returned the favor by winning the state championship. I'm just happy in the moment to be with Coach Dez, because I love him and Coach Hardaway.

"My life has been different ever since Dez came back. And with Penny, I became an even better person because he taught me discipline," the Mayor said. "I was getting in trouble with girls a lot. They told me girls will always be there, that I need to be focused and educated and to stay out of the streets. I'm so focused now because I know I can do something with my life."

Penny and Dez plotted for the new season at Lester. They lost seven eighth graders who were moving on to the high school ranks. But they had high hopes, thanks to Dez's son, Nick, the pint-sized veteran who was returning.

Lester repeated this year (2012–13 season), winning the state title in emphatic fashion, 62–18, to complete a 25-1 season. One of Robert Washington's brothers was named tournament MVP.

Dez continued to receive chemo twice a month. He never let anyone know the pain he constantly endured. He kept persevering and always had a smile on his face.

Penny didn't go away, either. He got more involved.

He formed Team Penny AAU squads to keep kids in the gym and off the streets during the dangerous summertime months. The teams range in age from grade school to early high school. Among his coaches: Dez, LaMarcus Golden, and former University of Arkansas star Todd Day.

More than five hundred kids benefited from the program

in the summer of 2012. Some got to travel to far-off places like Washington, D.C., Orlando, and Dallas.

"I can now spend more time working with kids, and less time worrying about places to play," Penny told reporters in late April. "I want to give them what I had. I want to give them a fighting chance."

The site of his newly refurbished gym was at Methodist University Hospital, the facility that helped save Desmond. The hospital offered the gym to Penny to keep inner-city kids active year-round.

The Lester players sat in folding chairs behind Penny, beaming as he spoke at the court's unveiling. Dez said it was only fitting the gym was at the hospital where he nearly died. "This is the same place he came to visit me," Dez said. "Now with this gym, I think it is great for the entire city."

On a wall near center court is Team Penny's motto: "All for One, One for All, All for Memphis."

Penny hired famed NBA shooting coach Buzz Braman—the Shot Doctor—to personally work with some of the city's top high school players, to improve their game and get them ranked in the top fifty players in the nation. Braman said he didn't quite understand the scope of Penny's involvement until he arrived in Memphis. Most big-time ballplayers lend their name to an organization and never do anything beyond collecting checks.

"He had told me he was doing something in Memphis," Braman said. "But I got here and was like 'Oh my God, this is not one kid.' He's taking over a void. I said to him, 'Do you realize what you're undertaking?' . . . I know the driving force with him is these kids: He doesn't want them to end up the way that a lot of people end up going in this town. A lot of these kids don't have a chance, and he's giving them a chance. He's not doing it for monetary reasons. In fact, he's donating a lot of dollars to this cause. And he's doing it for the betterment of the players and this town that he loves.

"This is him hands-on, taking the bull by the horns, trying to help the kids and trying to improve the quality of basketball. And help these kids become men. He's all in."

Penny hopes to break ground on Penny's FastBreak Courts in suburban Memphis in 2013. The $20 million facility would house seven basketball courts, including a two-thousand-seat arena, as well as an auditorium, a rehabilitation clinic, and classrooms to tutor kids. It would be located along a new bike and walking path to allow children easy access and encourage good exercise.

But the plan has stalled due to politics. Local Memphis elected officials have said no public funds will be made available unless the facility is built in the inner city. The *Memphis Commercial Appeal*'s editorial page backed the lawmakers.

"Money well spent," the headline blared. The editorial went on to say that the Shelby County Commission was "able to include extra money to help the homeless and to aid basketball star Anfernee 'Penny' Hardaway's efforts to build a youth sports facility, but only with the provision that the facility must be located in the inner city instead of in Cordova."

When I read that newspaper editorial, I wondered if anyone had bothered to ask Penny his reason for a suburban location. He told me he wants the facility located away from the inner city because it will allow the children to see life beyond their boundaries.

"What happened with me, I was in AAU and I'd have to drive out to the suburbs," Penny told me. "What that gave me: I started dreaming more. I started telling myself, 'I want to be in these nice neighborhoods. I don't want to be stuck in my neighborhood.' I'm hoping that by living in the neighborhood and going to the suburbs they can at least start dreaming, they can start seeing more things."

He said he is working on a plan to have shuttle buses available for kids who can't bicycle to the facility.

Dez said the politicians don't get it. "They don't understand that just taking the kids out of Binghampton for just a couple hours in the afternoon out to East Memphis is like going out of town for these kids." If Penny's FastBreak Courts is built in the suburbs, Dez said, the children will be exposed to "the big houses, the fancy cars, the nice restaurants, and a kid will start thinking, 'I want to live in this house one day.' That makes you want to work that much harder. But the politicians can't understand Penny's vision. They've never been in that predicament he was in, coming up through here. It's hard, man. It's hard growing up in this area. It ain't no cakewalk. For real."

Penny personally coached one AAU team of soon-to-be ninth graders. They finished fifth in the nation in a tournament held in Orlando, the city where Penny rose to fame. The rafters in the new Orlando arena remain bare. The Magic organization has never retired a jersey. Fans in recent years have called for Penny's No. 1 jersey to be the first—to honor the franchise's fifth-leading scorer, who took them to the title game in just his second season. As his original agents, the Poston brothers, predicted, Penny did win over the fans. Yet the Magic has always balked at the jersey retirement suggestions.

Penny doesn't let it bother him. He's got too many children dependent on him now. Too many lessons to instill.

Not everyone in Memphis is happy about his involvement. In the shady world of AAU basketball, "runners" act as intermediaries for agents and financial advisers. They deal only in cash. Coaches get their pockets lined with thousands of dollars. Players get bought and sold. On a summer afternoon, I sat in the stands watching Team Penny annihilate an opponent by about 40 points.

Two longtime Memphis AAU coaches sat nearby. The city's best players had naturally begun gravitating toward Penny and, by doing so, cut into their cash flow.

"I got twenty years invested in this," one of the coaches said. "And he just comes in here."

The other interrupted, "Everybody just loves the flavor of the day. It's *bullshit*! Just wait. He ain't gonna be in it for the long haul."

They didn't know who I was, or that I was listening in. It seemed to me like one more sign of Penny's importance—cutting through the corruption. I chuckled to myself that the two had better be glad Big Slaw Dog didn't hear their conversation. He would've pounded their faces. At a party to celebrate the Lester Lions, Big Slaw Dog had told me that what happened in the championship game was Penny's own life story personified: "Penny wanted it. He could've gave up when he got shot. Folks were talking about him, saying he's doing this or he's doing that. But he kept on going. He said, 'Ain't nobody gonna stop me. I know where I want to go.' Lester could've gave up in the championship. But that man showed so much love to them kids. He put it in their hearts, because they'd never had no real father around them who's treating them like he's doing. And they came all the way back and won. It lets folks know that when you get together, you can do a whole lotta things, instead of trying to fight or rob or take things from somebody."

Who would've known that a visit to an old friend in a hospital the year before would've resulted in all this? That Desmond's longing for team uniforms would push Penny to get so involved?

Penny told me he never would've thought ten years ago that his greatest basketball moment would come in retirement, with kids from his old neighborhood. But he's matured now, more reflective.

"It's not about the money that I made. I want people to say of my legacy: He's a person that really cared. I want them to know I really genuinely care about people's well-being and am trying to make a way for others to live out their dreams."

Asked what Lil Penny would say of what transpired on these courts, Penny broke into the high-pitched voice of his swashbuckling alter ego: "I told you my man was gonna come back. Everybody said he wasn't gonna come back. But I told you. I told you he was!"

He flashed his million-dollar smile. "Lil Penny would be bragging about me coming back to the neighborhood."

The Desmond Merriweather Trust Fund has been established to help pay for Desmond's continuing cancer treatment and to help establish college funds for the twelve team members of the 2012 Lester Middle championship team. Contributions can be made to:

The Desmond Merriweather Trust
Cumberland Trust and Investment Company, Trustee
700 Colonial Rd., Suite 101
Memphis, TN 38117

Acknowledgments

As a longtime fan of Memphis basketball, I've always been curious about the wrong path taken by so many of the players I worshipped growing up. It's something that has haunted me for years, as it has for so many others who love basketball in the city. *On These Courts* allowed me to explore those questions.

Many people helped me with their wisdom of Memphis hoops and insights through the course of writing this book. Most of all, a special thanks to Desmond Merriweather, who allowed me to stay in his apartment in the Hood to give me a full understanding of life and struggle in Binghampton. He took me to areas within Memphis that I feel confident saying few white people have ever been. I also went with him during one chemotherapy session to get a better understanding of his cancer fight. He trusted me enough to let me inside his world and tell the story of the Lester Lions on this grand scale. We stayed up many a night talking until 3 A.M. about what transpired during the 2012 season—even as the dope smoke from his neighbors next door wafted through his vents.

I want to thank Penny Hardaway for taking the time to speak with me and for allowing me special access inside the locker room during his AAU games. I still marvel that we first met at the age of fifteen at basketball camp in Kentucky and that our paths led us back together twenty-five years later. I can't say enough about his level of involvement in the lives of these young men. Just changing one of their lives is an extraordinary feat; his goal is to get all of them to college. Before he entered the scene at Lester, just graduating from high school was a lofty goal for most players.

I also had help from former Memphis Tiger greats Andre Turner, Chris Garner, and Anthony Douglas, all of whom took the time to speak candidly with me about their aspirations of changing the lives of young men in the inner city, of changing the view of Memphis basketball players as thugs. The same goes for Todd Day and LaMarcus Golden, who provided stories of what it was like growing up as star ballplayers in the city on the bluff. Rapper MJG also spoke to me about the importance of being a positive role model for the kids of Memphis. MJG and I even played a few games of horse on the courts of Lester.

More than anything, I can't thank the people of Binghampton enough. They rallied around the boys of Lester, and they showed me a peaceful side of Binghampton that never makes it in print. As I have said, I spoke with more than two hundred residents. To thank each one individually would be nearly impossible. But this book wouldn't have been possible if it weren't for Walter Casey, a stalwart of the Lester Community Center for the last four decades; for Big Slaw Dog; for the Memphis Duck; for Antoine Richardson; for Lester athletic director Demond Fason; for Rev. Larry Peoples; for teacher Monica Clark-Nunley; and for Reggie Green's grandmother Sheila Harris and Robert Washington's aunt Charity "Shree" Washington. The gang members of Binghampton were cordial and ingratiating to me, even willing to answer my endless questions. To them, I hope the truce holds for longer than just this season.

My mentor, Stephen Bloom at the University of Iowa, provided me with his time and guidance in helping me navigate my way through writing my first book. My eleventh-grade English teacher, Eva Jane Johnston, helped encourage me at difficult times to keep writing—that it was a story worth bringing to the world. My mother provided me with inspiration years ago, when in 1966 she taught with the first integrated teaching staff in Memphis history; her mother (my grandmother) accused her of sleeping with the principal and threatened to cut my mom from the family. Throughout this endeavor, I thought of my late paternal grandfather, Joseph Wayne Drash, an outspoken preacher in Birmingham, Alabama, from 1945 to 1955. During that span, my grandfather called for the end of segregation—a stand that resulted in police commissioner Bull Conner threatening him on many occasions and eventually running him out of town. "Twenty million American citizens, more than one-tenth of the population, are still struggling for their basic human rights. The struggle is not for the purpose of securing special privileges, but solely to obtain those fundamental rights that are guaranteed by our Constitution," my grandfather said in one of his early sermons. It's in his spirit that I write.

I dedicated the book to three friends from high school: Malcolm Montgomery, Macio "Float" Franklin, and Arvin Stewart, who taught me that friendships can span the railroad tracks in the South. My lifelong friend, Stephen Spears, also provided constant encouragement, pushing me to keep writing, even in those moments when I felt like giving up.

On the publishing side, I am indebted to my unflappable editor, Matthew Benjamin at Touchstone. He offered sound advice in shaping the narrative and was a constant advocate in the book's overall message. I feel blessed to have worked with him and look forward to future projects. My agent, John Rudolph at Dystel & Goderich Literary Management, was an aggressive pit bull who believed this story from the outset and fought hard on my behalf to bring this story to print.

At CNN Digital, I must thank my bosses—Meredith Artley, Manuel Perez, Jan Winburn, and Steve Goldberg—for allowing me the time off to focus solely on the book during the summer of 2012 and for encouraging me along the way. To Steve Goldberg, I must give a lot of credit. He helped edit the original story for the website, which led to this tremendous opportunity. His deft editing skills made that story sing. Without the help of Karin Hopkins and Bridget Evans, that story might never have come together. To them I will always be grateful.

The Grant Park Drinking Club—a band of misfit friends in Atlanta—provided valuable feedback, typically over many pints of Long Hammer IPA, at times when I suffered from writer's block. To those guys I owe a debt of gratitude.

My wife and children deserve special recognition. They tolerated my many trips back and forth to Memphis and supported me as I holed up for three months writing, often while neglecting them. With these pages they can now see a finished product, and I hope will agree that the effort put into this book was worthwhile. A long strange, wild, fantastic journey. That's what life is about.

A Note on Sourcing

I want to express my special gratitude to Penny Hardaway and Desmond Merriweather for allowing me access into their lives. The vast majority of locker room scenes come directly from video I was allowed to observe that was shot during the course of the season. The extended dialogue in many of the chapters is a result of watching the video and taking notes from what transpired. Each video was time-stamped as to the date and time they were shot. I matched those dates with the Lester Lions schedule, which allowed me to follow the progression of the season as it played out, even though I as a journalist came in at the end of the season. I spoke with more than two hundred people from the neighborhood, including Penny's relatives and friends, to get a better understanding of his upbringing, the neighborhood, and what this season meant to everyone in Binghampton. Those interviews helped to develop scenes in which no known video exists, but multiple people confirmed that what I've written did happen. In those cases, I paraphrased the scenes and only used brief quotes after at least two people confirmed what was said.

The video for the final game ended just as the comeback began. I pieced together the final moments from dozens of fans and players, from photos that showed the scoreboard during the comeback, and from local media recaps of the game (which varied wildly).

I would like to thank the entire community of Binghampton for allowing me a glimpse into life in the Hood. I will forever remember the great people of the BBB—Beautiful Black Binghampton.

Notes

Chapter 1: The Curse of the Assassination

7   *Kentucky won two national titles:* University of Kentucky sports information department, http://ukcc.uky.edu/cgi-bin/dynamo?maps .391+campus+0019.

10   *Anfernee was there:* Account provided by Michael Toney, May 2012.

12   *From 1970 to 1980:* U.S. Census Bureau, data compiled from 1970 to 1980 census.

13   *One in four people:* Tom Charlier, "Census Calls Memphis Poorest in Nation," *The Commercial Appeal,* September 23, 2011.

17   *Orange Mound, one of the first neighborhoods:* Laura Nickas, *The Tennessee Encyclopedia of History and Culture,* http://tennesseecncyclopedia.net/ entry.php?rec=1638.

Chapter 2: Millions to a Penny

21   *Brick struck:* Ralph Wiley, "A Daunting Proposition," *Sports Illustrated,* August 21, 1991.

22   *Louise and Sylvester Hardaway:* Ralph Wiley, "A Daunting Proposition," *Sports Illustrated,* August 21, 1991.

22   *The walls in the Hardaway home:* Ralph Wiley, "A Daunting Proposition," *Sports Illustrated,* August 21, 1991.

25   *"I'd be standing at the door":* Ron Higgins, "Superlatives Pouring in on Hardaway," *The Commercial Appeal,* October 29, 1989.

34   *Nike/ABCD basketball camp:* Barry Temkin, "Aiming Higher Than the Rim," *Chicago Tribune,* July 16, 1989.

35   *Forty percent of those:* Barry Temkin, "Aiming Higher Than the Rim," *Chicago Tribune,* July 16, 1989.

36   *At Memphis State, Tim Sumner:* Celeste Williams, "Athletes Excel Off

the Court at MSU's Academic Center," *Memphis Business Journal*, September 10, 1990.

38   *"The legend has just been born":* Jim Valvano, ESPN, November 29, 1991.

38   *He finished with 18 points:* University of Memphis sports information department.

39   *"It doesn't impress me":* Lynn Zinser, "Hardaway's Last Stand," *The Commercial Appeal*, March 11, 1993.

39   *"He was absolutely spectacular":* GoTigersGo.com, The Official Website of Memphis athletics, http://www.gotigersgo.com/sports/m-baskbl/archive/101899aab.html.

40   *Reporter Craig Sager:* TNT broadcast, June 30, 1993.

40   *"We're going to play great":* Ron Higgins, "Hardaway to Sign with Orlando for $65 Million," *The Commercial Appeal*, October 7, 1993.

41   *Carl and Kevin Poston*: Selena Roberts, "No Play, Plenty of Pay Are OK with Hardaway," *The Orlando Sentinel*, September 2, 1993.

41   *$65 million deal:* Ron Higgins, "Hardaway to Sign with Orlando for $65 Million," *The Commercial Appeal*, October 7, 1993.

42   *He raised $100,000:* Mike DeCourcy, "Penny's Classic Makes $100,000 for Charities," *The Commercial Appeal*, July 28, 1995.

42   *He scored 71 points*: David Williams, "Penny Pours in 71 Points," *The Commercial Appeal*, August 18, 1996.

43   *Converse offered:* Selena Roberts, "No Play, Plenty of Pay Are OK with Hardaway," *The Orlando Sentinel*, September 2, 1993.

44   *"It really keeps me":* Ron Higgins, "One Penny Is Worth More Than Thousands to Charity," *The Commercial Appeal*, December 31, 1995.

44   *"My first day here":* Ron Higgins, "Amid Bomb, Birthday, Sudden Lack of Shaq, Penny Shines at the Games," *The Commercial Appeal*, August 4, 1996.

47   *He was informed:* Commercial Appeal Press Service, "Unlucky Penny: Hardaway Waived by Miami," *The Commercial Appeal*, December 13, 2007.

Chapter 3: The Soldier

54   *"He's a man-child":* Larry Starks, "Merriweather Ignites East," *The Commercial Appeal*, January 27, 1993.

Chapter 4: A Birthday Bash

63   *Six people, ranging in age:* Trevor Aaronson, "Lester Victims Shot Many Times," *The Commercial Appeal*, June 27, 2008.

Chapter 6: Reshaping Boys

87   *When his eleven-month-old daughter:* Geoff Calkins, "Wright Tragedy Stuns Fans, Friends," *The Commercial Appeal,* July 28, 2010; and Dan Wolken, "Gone Too Soon," *The Commercial Appeal,* August 5, 2010.

87   *"Germantown 911":* Germantown Police Department, July 2010.

88   *Lorenzen lay bleeding:* Germantown Police Department, July 2010

89   *His ex-wife, Sherra Wright, told police:* Germantown and Collierville Police Departments, July 2010.

89   *The FBI in 2008*: "Police: Wright Died from Gunshot Wound," The Associated Press, July 30, 2010.

90   *"I sometimes look at the programs":* Greg Garber, "Finch: 'When the Basketball Is Over, Reality Sets In,'" ESPN.com, June 4, 2001, http://espn.go.com/gen/s/2001/0604/1209377.html.

91   *"What people don't realize":* Mike Lopresti, "'85 Memphis State Run Went From Triumph to Tragedy," *USA Today,* April 3, 2008.

91   *Michael Heisley, the owner:* Dan Wolken, "Gone Too Soon," *The Commercial Appeal,* August 5, 2010.

91   *"Every other minute":* Mitch Abramson, "Memphis Murder Mystery," *New York Daily News,* August 8, 2010.

Chapter 9: Academics First

124   *William Charles Lester was an architect:* Norton Rosengarten, "W.C. Lester Has Designed Buildings For Many Purposes in a Dozen States," *The Memphis Press-Scimitar,* October 8, 1935; and Staff, "W.C. Lester, 80, Dies At Home," *The Commercial Appeal,* December 12, 1960.

126   *In 2010, just 2 percent:* Tennessee Department of Education, http://www.greatschools.org/modperl/achievement/tn/968.

126   *In the 1980s, Lester was one of five:* Christine Arpe Gang, "The Classroom of Tomorrow Is Here Today," *The Commercial Appeal,* August 2, 1987.

127   *In 2001, with students in every grade struggling:* Wayne Risher, "Literacy Is Key, Says New Lester Principal," *The Commercial Appeal,* December 20, 2001.

Chapter 11: Truce

149   *The GDs were the first:* Staff, "Big 4: Gangster Disciples, Vice Lords, Crips, Bloods," *The Commercial Appeal,* March 23, 2008.

149 *"You've got a lot of young kids":* Beth Warren, "Memphis Agencies Unite to Tackle Gangs," *The Commercial Appeal,* July 23, 2012.

155 *Lester Street murders:* Trevor Aaronson, "Lester Victims Shot Many Times," *The Commercial Appeal,* June 27, 2008.

Chapter 12: Know Your Friends

162 *"I kept thinking":* Ron Higgins, "Hardaway Shot in Foot," *The Commercial Appeal,* April 30, 1991.

162 *"He was very fortunate":* Ron Higgins, "Hardaway Shot in Foot," *The Commercial Appeal,* April 30, 1991.

163 *"It ricocheted right":* Ron Higgins, "Hardaway Shot in Foot," *The Commercial Appeal,* April 30, 1991.

163 *"The Good Lord was":* Ron Higgins, "Hardaway Shot in Foot," *The Commercial Appeal,* April 30, 1991.

163 *Indicted by a federal grand jury:* Ron Higgins, "Man with Hardaway Faces Trial for Cocaine," *The Commercial Appeal,* May 1, 1991; Chris Conley, "Megajam Head Agrees to Plea Deal," *The Commercial Appeal,* January 7, 1992; and Chris Conley, "Megajam Records Owner Sentenced," *The Commercial Appeal,* May 23, 1992.

163 *"I've grown up knowing Terry":* Ron Higgins, "Hardaway Gears for Debut," *The Commercial Appeal,* July 28, 1991.

163 *"My kids have to":* Ron Higgins, "Man with Hardaway Faces Trial for Cocaine," *The Commercial Appeal,* May 1, 1991.

Chapter 18: The Enforcers

209 *"It was just business":* Beth Warren, "Trial Offers View of Memphis' Drug Lords," *The Commercial Appeal,* "February 26, 2012.

212 *East has stood:* The History of East High School, The East High Alumni Page, http://www.easthigh.org/fullhist.html.

Chapter 19: Championship Time

218 *57–50 loss:* Thomas Harding, "Fairley Tops Westwood," *The Commercial Appeal,* February 29, 1992.

218 *Nominated as a McDonald's All-American:* Staff, "Shelby-Metro Players McDonald Nominees," *The Commercial Appeal,* February 10, 1993.

Chapter 20: Championships That Got Away

224 *"Everybody kept saying"*: Mike Wise, "1995 NBA Playoffs: Do you believe in the Magic? The Indiana Pacers Do," *The New York Times,* June 5, 1995.

225 *"I remember players"*: Ron Higgins, "Penny's Dream Starts Tonight," *The Commercial Appeal,* June 7, 1995.

225 *Horace Grant showed off:* "Headliners," *Orlando Sentinel,* June 8, 1995.

225 *"He can do it all"*: Wendy E. Lane, "Centers of Attention," The Associated Press, June 6, 1995.

225 *"The Orlando Magic were labeled"*: Bob Costas, NBC, June 7, 1995.

226 *"At the beginning of the season"*: Shaquille O'Neal, NBC interview, June 7, 1995.

226 *"The story here is this"*: Bob Costas, NBC, June 7, 1995.

227 *"Olajuwon, yes!"*: Marv Albert, NBC, June 7, 1995.

228 *"And for Hardaway"*: Marv Albert, NBC, June 7, 1995.

228 *"Hakeem was running"*: Bill Walton, NBC, June 7, 1995.

228 *"Foul called"*: Marv Albert, NBC, June 7, 1995.

229 *Make Room for Anderson:* Gary Shelton, "Make Room for Anderson in Next Frame," *St. Petersburg Times,* June 7, 1995.

229 *"Anderson missing on both"*: Marv Albert, NBC, June 7, 1995.

230 *"And he misses four straight"*: Marv Albert, NBC, June 7, 1995.

230 *"He's been on fire"*: Marv Albert, NBC, June 7, 1995.

230 *"Kenny Smith says forget it"*: Bill Walton, NBC, June 7, 1995.

230 *"Drexler driving"*: Joe McConnell, NBA Radio, June 7, 1995.

231 *"One night, one game, one simple shot"*: Fran Blinebury, "Brick by Brick, Anderson's Misses Tore Down Magic" Yahoo! Sports, June 8, 2009, http://sports.yahoo.com/nba/news?slug=ys-andersonmagic060809.

Epilogue

250 *"I can now spend more time"*: Lela Garlington, "New Home Court Has Its Advantages," *The Commercial Appeal,* April 25, 2012.

251 *"This is the same place"*: Lela Garlington, "New Home Court Has Its Advantages," *The Commercial Appeal,* April 25, 2012.

252 *"Money well spent"*: Editorial, *The Commercial Appeal,* May 30, 2012.

INDEX